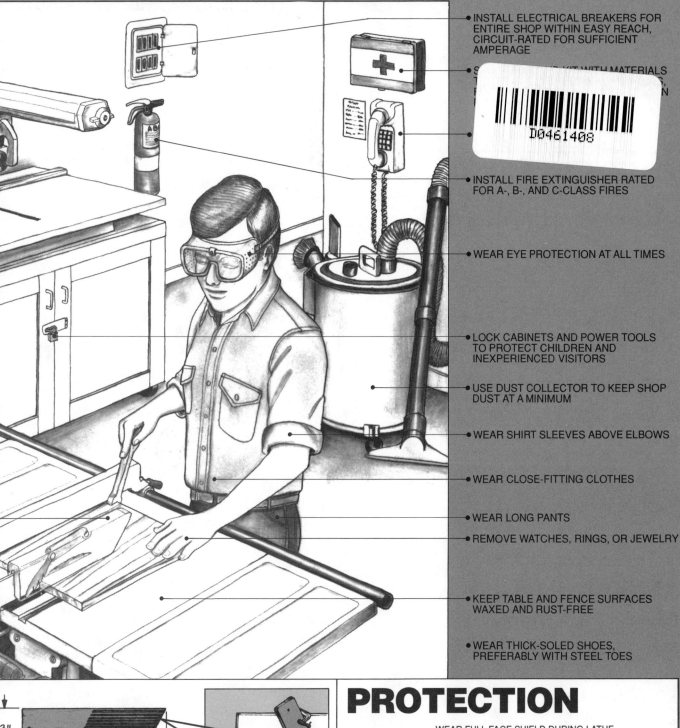

- INSTALL ELECTRICAL BREAKERS FOR ENTIRE SHOP WITHIN EASY REACH, CIRCUIT-RATED FOR SUFFICIENT AMPERAGE

- S̶̶̶̶̶ ̶̶̶̶ ̶̶̶ KIT WITH MATERIALS

- INSTALL FIRE EXTINGUISHER RATED FOR A-, B-, AND C-CLASS FIRES

- WEAR EYE PROTECTION AT ALL TIMES

- LOCK CABINETS AND POWER TOOLS TO PROTECT CHILDREN AND INEXPERIENCED VISITORS

- USE DUST COLLECTOR TO KEEP SHOP DUST AT A MINIMUM

- WEAR SHIRT SLEEVES ABOVE ELBOWS

- WEAR CLOSE-FITTING CLOTHES

- WEAR LONG PANTS

- REMOVE WATCHES, RINGS, OR JEWELRY

- KEEP TABLE AND FENCE SURFACES WAXED AND RUST-FREE

- WEAR THICK-SOLED SHOES, PREFERABLY WITH STEEL TOES

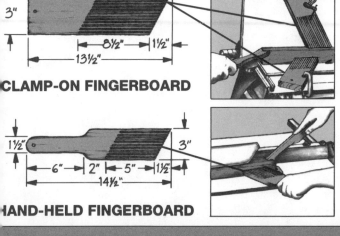

3"
8½" — 1½"
13½"

CLAMP-ON FINGERBOARD

1½"
6" — 2" — 5" — 1½"
3"
14½"

HAND-HELD FINGERBOARD

PROTECTION

WEAR FULL FACE SHIELD DURING LATHE TURNING, ROUTING, AND OTHER OPERATIONS THAT MAY THROW CHIPS

WEAR DUST MASK DURING SANDING AND SAWING

WEAR VAPOR MASK DURING FINISHING

WEAR SAFETY GLASSES OR GOGGLES AT ALL TIMES

WEAR RUBBER GLOVES FOR HANDLING DANGEROUS CHEMICALS

WEAR EAR PROTECTORS DURING ROUTING, PLANING, AND LONG, CONTINUOUS POWER TOOL OPERATION

THE WORKSHOP COMPANION™

GLUING AND CLAMPING

TECHNIQUES FOR BETTER WOODWORKING

by Nick Engler

Rodale Press
Emmaus, Pennsylvania

Printed in the United States of America on acid-free ∞, recycled ♲ paper

If you have any questions or comments concerning this book, please write:
  Rodale Press
  Book Readers' Service
  33 East Minor Street
  Emmaus, PA 18098

About the Author: Nick Engler is an experienced woodworker, writer, and teacher. He worked as a luthier for many years, making traditional American musical instruments before he founded *Hands On!* magazine. Today, he contributes to several woodworking magazines and teaches woodworking at the University of Cincinnati. He has written more than 30 books.

Series Editor: Jeff Day
Editors: Bob Moran
          Roger Yepsen
Copy Editor: Carolyn Mandarano
Graphic Designer: Linda Watts
Illustrator: Mary Jane Favorite
Master Craftsman: Jim McCann
Photographer: Karen Callahan
Cover Photographer: Mitch Mandel
Proofreader: Hue Park
Indexer: Beverly Bremer
Typesetting by Computer Typography, Huber Heights, Ohio
Interior and endpaper illustrations by Mary Jane Favorite
Produced by Bookworks, Inc., West Milton, Ohio

Library of Congress Cataloging-in-Publication Data

Engler, Nick.
    Gluing and clamping/by Nick Engler.
        p.   cm. — (The workshop companion)
    Includes index.
    ISBN 0–87596–580–6   hardcover
    1. Woodwork.   2. Gluing.   3. Clamps (Engineering).
      I. Title   II. Series:
Engler, Nick.   Workshop companion.
TT185.E53   1993
683'.08—dc20   93–10486
                                CIP

      6 8 10 9 7 5   hardcover

Special Thanks to:

Franklin International
George W. Ritter, Ph.D.
Jeffery B. Shumaker
Columbus, Ohio

Nemeth Engineering
Crestwood, Kentucky

Paxton Lumber Company
Jeff Arnold
Cincinnati, Ohio

Shopsmith, Inc.
Dayton, Ohio

Wertz Hardware
West Milton, Ohio

CONTENTS

TECHNIQUES

PROJECTS

TECHNIQUES

1

A CLOSE LOOK AT GLUES

One tongue-in-cheek definition of woodworking describes it as the act of cutting larger boards into smaller boards, then gluing them back together again in the hopes of creating something useful. Those of us who have worked wood long enough know that this statement, although whimsical, has as much truth as humor. The vast majority of woodworking projects require some gluing — the pieces are bonded together to make the completed project stronger than it would be if it were carved from a single piece of wood. The glue's ability to bond wood infuses woodworkers with the hope that they might create something useful from small pieces they cut.

But most craftsmen take glue for granted. They know so little about how it works that gluing might as well be sorcery. Just reach for a bottle of magic elixir, smear it on the wooden surfaces to be assembled, press them together for a short time, and presto! — they're bonded. However, there's a lot more to gluing two pieces of wood together than one might suspect. A deeper understanding of this process can help you avoid common pitfalls and make stronger, more durable glue joints.

THE ANATOMY OF A GLUE JOINT

A *glue joint* attaches the surface of one piece of wood to another. (Glue chemists refer to the wood pieces as *adherends* and prefer to call the glue an *adhesive*.) This is not just a surface attachment; the adhesive penetrates a small distance into the wood, forming an *interphase* in each adjoining piece. *(SEE FIGURE 1-1.)* When the adhesive cures, the joint will not break unless you apply a great deal of force to it. In fact, the load from the force or *stress* that you put on one piece of wood is transferred across the joint to the second, as if the two pieces were one. *(SEE FIGURE 1-2.)* If wood is glued together properly, a glue joint should be stronger than the wood itself!

The strength of the joint depends on two properties — the *cohesion* of the glue and its *adhesion* to the wood. Cohesion refers to the bonds within a single substance. The glue molecules in the glue line *cohere* to one another. Adhesion refers to bonds between unlike substances — in this case, between the glue and the wood. The glue *adheres* to the wood in two ways, through *mechanical adhesion* and *specific adhesion*.

Mechanical adhesion develops when the glue penetrates pores and cell cavities in the wood, then hardens around these intricate structures. While this occurs at a microscopic level, specific adhesion takes place at a molecular level — the wood molecules and the glue molecules attract one another because of their opposite electrical charges. Specific adhesion is a great deal stronger than mechanical adhesion, but there are more mechanical bonds in a typical glue joint than there are specific bonds. So both types of adhesion contribute roughly equally to the strength of the joint.

Several other important factors influence the relative strength of the glue bond:

- Type of wood or wood product
- Type of adhesive
- Environmental conditions in which the glue cures
- Total area of the surfaces to be bonded
- Orientation of the wood grain
- Assembly technique
- Fit of the joint

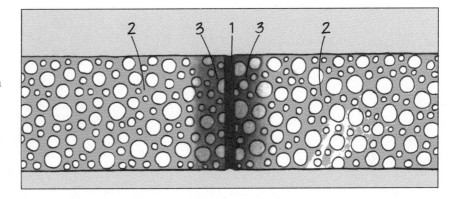

1-1 When you apply glue or *adhesive* (1) to two pieces of wood or *adherends* (2) and then press them together, the adhesive penetrates a short distance into the wood, forming an *interphase* (3) in each piece. These interphases are essential to the strength of the glue joint, since this is where the glue and the wood *adhere* to one another.

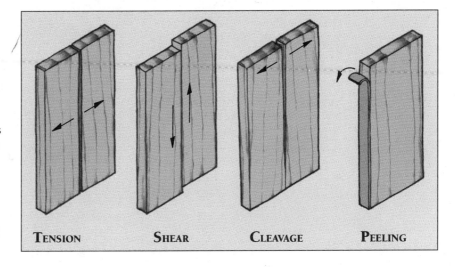

1-2 A glue joint must withstand stress, transferring the load across the glue line so both pieces of wood share it. The four common types of stress that a glue joint must withstand are *tension,* in which the pieces are pulled apart perpendicular to the glue line; *shear,* in which the pieces are pushed past one another parallel to the glue line; *cleavage,* in which the joint is pulled apart a little at a time, starting at one edge; and *peeling,* in which a thin, flexible piece of wood is peeled from another.

TENSION   SHEAR   CLEAVAGE   PEELING

Of these, perhaps the most important factor is the fit of the joint. To form a strong bond, the wood surfaces must contact one another *intimately* all along the joint. In other words, each wood surface must remain in close contact with the other while the glue cures. When cured, the glue line should be thin and uniform.

Gaps or voids in the glue line weaken the joint, as do areas where the glue is too thick. The strongest glue joints are no thicker than a piece of typewriter paper (.002 to .003 inch), and are uniform throughout the length and breadth of the joint.

FILLING GAPS WITH GLUE

Perhaps the most common reason that glue joints fail is that the wood surfaces fit poorly, leaving gaps and voids between the adjoining wood parts. In fact, many inexperienced woodworkers try to fill voids in poorly made joints with glue. In doing so, they are depending on the cohesion of the glue (rather than its adhesion to the wood) to hold the joint together.

Unfortunately, most glues are poor gap fillers. Glues are formulated from resins and solvents. When the glue cures, the solvent evaporates or disperses into the wood, leaving only the resin behind. As it does so, the glue loses much of its bulk and shrinks. The voids and gaps reappear and — because the glue line is broken and uneven — the joint is very weak.

Some craftsmen attempt to solve this problem by mixing the glue with sawdust and using the resulting paste to fill gaps. This is only a partial solution at best. The solvent in many popular woodworking glues is water, which causes the sawdust to swell. Then when the glue dries, the sawdust shrinks and the gaps appear again.

If you're determined to fill gaps with glue, there are four effective techniques:

■ Use epoxy cement to secure the joint. Epoxy has an extremly high proportion of resins and shrinks very little. Also, the cohesion of an epoxy film is relatively strong.

■ Mix water-based glues with substances that won't expand, such as silica (powdered quartz), rottenstone, or talc.

■ Mix sawdust with a glue that doesn't have a water base, such as model cement. This will prevent the sawdust from expanding.

■ Assemble the ill-fitting joint using *slightly* more glue than you would for one that fits properly. While the glue is still wet, press small wedges or

slivers of wood into the gaps. (*Don't* pound them in; you'll crush the wood fibers.) Carefully choose and arrange these wedges so the color and grain direction match the adjoining pieces of wood. When the glue dries, sand the wedges flush with the wood surface.

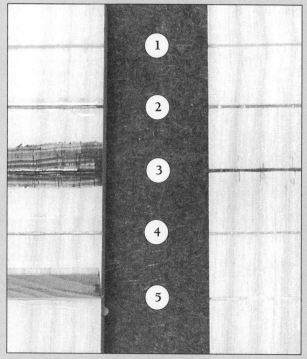

The saw kerfs in these blocks of wood were filled with aliphatic (yellow) glue (1), epoxy cement (2), polyvinyl (white) glue mixed with rottenstone (3), model cement mixed with sawdust (4), and a small wooden wedge, secured with glue (5). As you can see, the wooden wedge does the best job of filling the gap.

ADHESIVE TYPES AND PROPERTIES

Glues are simple concoctions, with just two major ingredients — a *resin* (the glue solid) and a *vehicle* or *solvent* (to keep the resin liquid until it's applied). Some water-based glues may also include an *emulsifier* to keep the resin suspended in the water. Glues cure in several different ways. Most simply harden as the solvent dissipates. Others change chemically — the molecules cross-link, forming a strong, intricate matrix. (Chemists call this *polymerization.*) A few glues are applied hot and harden as they cool.

GLUE PROPERTIES

In addition to the way it cures, each glue formula has characteristics or *properties* that suit it to specific woodworking operations. These properties fall into two categories — those that control the glue's *workability* and those that determine its *durability*.

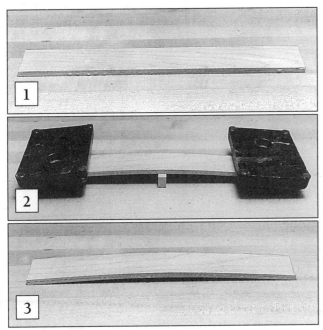

1-3 Some glues will *creep* — that is, they will allow the adjoining wood parts to shift slightly under stress. These two long, thin boards were glued together face-to-face with polyvinyl (white) glue and allowed to cure for 48 hours (1). Then the assembly was balanced on a small block and the ends were weighted (2). After two weeks, the glue has crept and the wood remains bent even without the weights (3).

The working properties are:

■ *Shelf or pot life* — Most ready-to-use glues have a certain shelf life. After this expires, their adhesive quality begins to degrade. Glues that must be mixed before using have a pot life, after which they also become unusable.

■ *Open assembly time* — Also called working time, this is the amount of time you have to spread the glue, assemble the parts, align them, and apply the clamps before the glue begins to cure. If the glue cures partially before you've clamped the parts together, it won't penetrate the wood properly and the resulting glue joint will be weak.

■ *Closed assembly time* — This is also called set time or clamp time and refers to the length of time you must leave the assembly in the clamps until the bonds develop sufficiently for you to remove them.

■ *Cure time* — The length of time required for the glue bond to attain full strength. Only at this point is the glue cured or hardened sufficiently so the joint can be machined or sanded.

■ *Sandability* — Refers to how easily the glue can be sanded and whether or not it tends to clog or *load* the sandpaper.

■ *Working temperature range* — You must apply the glue within this temperature range for it to cure properly. In some cases, a glue won't cure at all when applied outside this range.

 FOR YOUR INFORMATION

Although *tack time* is not usually counted as a working property, it is an important characteristic. This is the time it takes for the glue to just *begin* to set. If you align the boards and hold them together in your hands for a few minutes until the glue develops sufficient *tack,* they will usually stay together and remain aligned long enough for you to apply the clamps.

The properties that contribute to a glue's durability are:

■ *Strength* — The strength of a glue joint refers to its ability to withstand all types of stress.

■ *Creep* — Some glue resins never harden completely, remaining elastic. When put under constant stress — from the wood expanding and contracting, gravity, or pressure — the glue will change shape very slowly, allowing the adjoining wood parts to shift, or creep, out of alignment. (*SEE FIGURE 1-3.*)

■ *Water resistance* — This is a measure of whether the glue can be dissolved by water and how quickly the joint will weaken and fail when exposed to it.

■ *Chemical resistance* — Just as some glues can be dissolved by water, they may also be dissolved or weakened by chemicals that are commonly used in woodworking — finishing solvents such as alcohol, mineral spirits, lacquer thinner, and so on.

■ *Heat resistance* — Many glue resins have a thermoplastic quality — that is, they turn liquid (lose their coherence) when heated. Heat resistance is a measure of how much heat must be applied to weaken the glue joint.

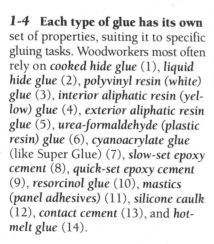

FOR YOUR INFORMATION

In addition to workability and durability, all glues have another important property — *cost.* There are enormous differences in the prices you pay for equal volumes of various glues. It may be that a glue with all the right working properties and sufficient durability is not economical for a large project. If economy is important, take the cost of the material into consideration when choosing a glue.

TYPES OF GLUE

Glues are classified according to the resin in their formula. There are many different glue resins, too many to discuss here. For our purposes, we'll consider only those adhesives that can be purchased through hardware stores, lumberyards, or mail-order woodworking suppliers. *(SEE FIGURE 1-4.)* These fall into four categories.

One-part glues usually come ready to use in a container and can be applied to the wood with no preparation. A few, however, come in powdered form and must be mixed with water. The most common choices are:

■ *Cooked hide glue* is made from natural resin boiled down from animal hooves, hides, bones, and sinews. This is one of the oldest glues known and is still a favorite among traditional craftsmen for its quick tack time and superior holding ability. It's sold as a powder or small beads, and it must be mixed with water and heated to between 125° and 140°F in a *glue pot*. *(SEE FIGURE 1-5.)* Hide glue is applied hot, using a brush. It does not keep well in liquid form and must be mixed fresh each day.

■ *Liquid hide glue* is made with the same natural resins as cooked hide glue, plus additives that keep it from spoiling and allow you to apply it at room temperature. It's weaker than cooked hide glue, but has an extremely long open assembly time. Unlike its cooked cousin, it can be used for complex glue-ups when you need a few extra minutes to assemble all the parts.

1-4 **Each type of glue has its own** set of properties, suiting it to specific gluing tasks. Woodworkers most often rely on *cooked hide glue* (1), *liquid hide glue* (2), *polyvinyl resin (white) glue* (3), *interior aliphatic resin (yellow) glue* (4), *exterior aliphatic resin glue* (5), *urea-formaldehyde (plastic resin) glue* (6), *cyanoacrylate glue* (like Super Glue) (7), *slow-set epoxy cement* (8), *quick-set epoxy cement* (9), *resorcinol glue* (10), *mastics (panel adhesives)* (11), *silicone caulk* (12), *contact cement* (13), and *hot-melt glue* (14).

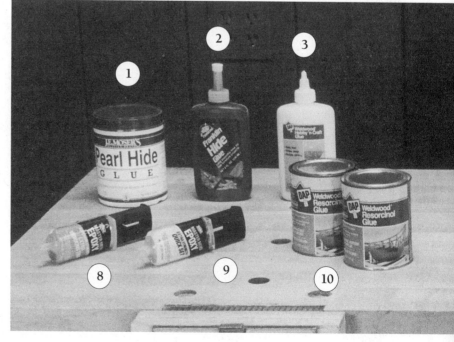

1-5 Although there are electric glue pots available to regulate the heat of cooked hide glue, it's not necessary to buy one, especially if you only use this kind of glue occasionally. Instead, cook the glue in a *double boiler* on an electric hot plate, as shown. Monitor the temperature with a candy thermometer.

■ *Polyvinyl resin glue* (also called white glue) is made from a synthetic polyvinyl acetate (PVA) resin. This is a strong general-purpose woodworking adhesive, with adequate open assembly time for all but the most complex glue-ups. Unfortunately, it's somewhat runny and dribbles off vertical surfaces before you can assemble them. After the glue has cured, it clogs the sandpaper when you sand it. Still, it's an extremely useful adhesive when you need extra open assembly time.

■ *Aliphatic resin glue* (also called yellow glue or carpenter's glue) is also made with PVA resin, but the formula has been modified to render it less runny and more sandable. This makes it the preferred general

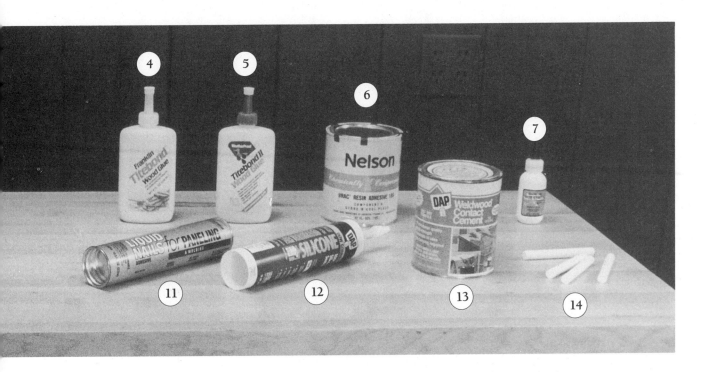

adhesive for many woodworkers. It also sets faster, which speeds the assembly of most projects but, unfortunately, shortens the open assembly time. It's available in both interior and exterior (weatherproof) forms. When cured, the interior version is water-soluble, but the weatherproof version is water-resistant — that is, it will hold together through a long, soaking thunderstorm, but not if you submerge it in your pool.

■ *Urea-formaldehyde glue* (also called plastic resin glue) is made with a synthetic plastic resin, comes in powdered form, and must be mixed with water before it can be applied. Because this glue contains formaldehyde, its vapors are toxic, so it must be used with adequate ventilation. It has long open and closed

assembly times, but can be cured immediately with radio frequency. *(SEE FIGURE 1-6.)* When cured, it turns a tan color that blends with the wood and leaves an almost invisible glue line.

■ *Cyanoacrylate glue* (like the Super Glue brand) is made with an acrylic resin that hardens almost immediately when it contacts minute amounts of moisture in the air or on the gluing surface. It works best on nonporous surfaces that mate perfectly and is not the best choice for general woodworking. However, a few formulations are mixed to work with wood, and these are useful for repairs and small tasks. Make sure the label on the container mentions that the product will bond wood. *(SEE FIGURE 1-7.)*

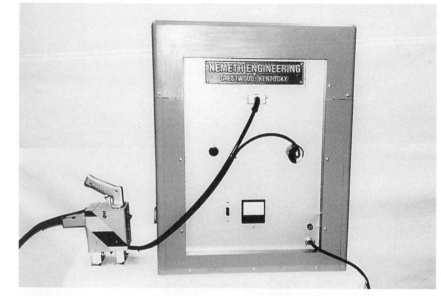

1-6 Plastic resin glue is a favorite among professional cabinetmakers because of its flexible working times. It has long open and closed assembly times, but once you have the pieces clamped up, you can cure the glue quickly with radio frequency (RF), shortening the closed time to a few minutes. RF gluing tools emit high-frequency, low-voltage radio waves that heat the glue molecules (but not the wood) and cause the adhesive to harden almost immediately. Unfortunately, RF tools are extremely expensive. The hand-held version shown costs several thousand dollars. *Photo courtesy of Nemeth Engineering, Crestwood, Kentucky.*

1-7 Cyanoacrylate glues are too finicky and too expensive for general woodworking, but they are useful for small tasks. Turners and woodcarvers frequently use them to repair breaks, reattach small wood chips, and harden *punk* (partially decayed) wood. Inlay artists use them to secure precious metals, mother-of-pearl, and abalone to wood. They can also be used to attach wooden plugs and patches, as long as the repair part isn't too large and mates perfectly with the surrounding wood surface.

Two-part glues have two separate components — a resin and a hardener, or *catalyst,* — that must be mixed before the glues can be applied. They include:

■ *Epoxy cement* is made from epoxy and polyamine resin, and is commonly available in two forms — slow set and quick set. There is a large difference between the working times of the two types. After mixing the resin and the catalyst, the closed assembly time of the quick-set epoxy is about five minutes, while the slow-set type takes up to four hours. There are also special formulations available for gluing oily woods, for gluing at low temperatures, and to adjust the color, texture, and viscosity of the epoxy. All forms are extremely strong and waterproof. Unlike other glues, epoxy requires no clamping pressure to form a strong bond, so it's a good choice for assemblies that are difficult to clamp up. All these characteristics make epoxy the most versatile of the woodworking adhesives. Unfortunately, it's also one of the more expensive.

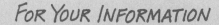

FOR YOUR INFORMATION

Some ratings systems don't classify epoxy as waterproof. The reason has nothing to do with water — all epoxies are unaffected by moisture. It has to do with the test method — the glue is *boiled* in water. Epoxy fails because it softens at 160°F.

■ *Resorcinol glue* is made from resorcinol and phenolresorcinol resins that come in liquid form, while the catalyst is usually a powder. It has long working times, is the strongest glue commonly available, and is completely waterproof. These properties make it the best choice for outdoor projects. However, the glue dries to a dark red-brown color, making the glue lines stand out in most woods. (*SEE FIGURE 1-8.*)

Elastomer adhesives, when cured, remain flexible. They can be deformed when stressed, but will return to their original shape when the stress is removed. They are normally very thick before they cure and are usually spread with a brush, spatula, or caulking gun. Your options are these:

■ *Mastics,* such as panel adhesives, are made with latex, rubber, and similar resins. They normally come in tubes and must be squeezed onto the wood. The glue line remains thick, and the cured adhesive is almost impossible to sand, which makes mastics unsuitable for fine woodworking. However, they will hold even when surfaces are rough and don't fit precisely. This makes them extremely useful for construction, finish carpentry, and architectural projects.

■ *Silicone caulk* is made from synthetic rubber, comes in a tube, and must be squeezed onto the wood. As with mastics, the glue line remains thick and is very difficult to sand. However, silicone caulk is very useful for bonding nonporous materials, such as glass or tile, to wood. It's also completely waterproof. (*SEE FIGURE 1-9.*)

1-8 Resorcinol glue is extremely strong and completely waterproof, making it a favorite for projects that must endure moisture in the kitchen, bathroom, or out-of-doors. The glue line dries to a dark red-brown and is highly visible. But if you're creative, you can use this in your design. For example, the pieces of wood in this project are delineated by their glue lines. If the craftsman had used a less-visible glue, the laminations might look indistinct and muddy.

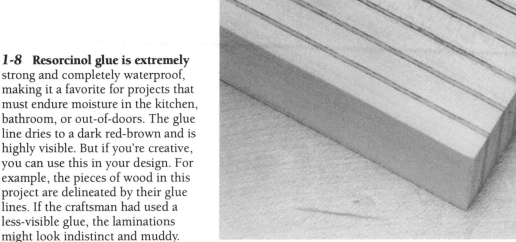

■ *Contact cement* is made from neoprene rubber and is used to secure veneers, plastic laminates, leather, and other thin materials to wood. This particular glue is applied to *both* surfaces, then allowed to dry for about 10 to 15 minutes before the parts are joined to bond them on contact. It's available in both petrochemical-based and water-based forms. The vapors are toxic and the petrochemical variety is *extremely* flammable, so both forms must be used with ventilation.

Thermoplastic glues change from a solid to a liquid when they are heated. They are applied hot, then harden as they cool:

■ *Hot-melt glue* is made from polyethylene and polyvinyl resins. It comes in sticks, which are heated and applied with a special gun. (*SEE FIGURE 1-10.*) The glue sets as soon as it cools. Because the open assembly time is measured in seconds, it's suitable only for gluing one joint at a time, and these must be no more complex than a rabbet or dado. However, hot-melt glue is useful for tacking pieces of wood together quickly. Some craftsmen use it for test fitting — "spot welding" the parts together temporarily with hot-melt glue, then disassembling the project with a heat gun.

1-9 Although silicone caulk is not used extensively in fine woodworking, craftsmen find it useful for specific tasks such as securing glass in a frame or keeping panels from rattling. Here a pane of glass is glued in a door frame before the wooden molding is nailed in place. Because the caulk is an elastomer, it will allow the wood frame to expand and contract while continuing to hold the glass so it won't rattle. **Note:** Silicone won't hold paint, varnish, or any other finishing material; so be careful not to get the caulk on surfaces that you intend to finish.

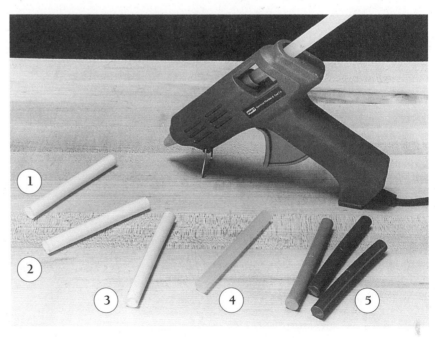

1-10 There are several types of hot-melt glue available, each formulated for a specific use — *general-purpose adhesive* (1), *wood adhesive* (2), *caulk/sealer* (3), *ceramic and glass adhesive* (4), and various colors of *craft adhesive* (5). You can also purchase various tips for your glue gun to make it easier to apply the glue to different types of surfaces.

CHOOSING THE GLUE

The adhesive you choose for a specific gluing task depends on the properties you require. To help decide which of these properties are the most important, ask yourself:

■ How and where will you assemble the project?
■ What wood or wood product will you use?
■ How will you use the assembled project?

How and where will you assemble the project? Your shop environment is critical; most glues won't set properly above or below certain temperatures. Aliphatic resin glue, for instance, turns white and brittle below 45°F. Many other glues fail above 100°F. The best temperature range for all common woodworking glues is about 70° to 80°F.

Some glues are affected by high humidity. Liquid hide glues and other water-based adhesives often take longer to cure when the weather is humid. Craftsmen who live in humid areas often have trouble storing cyanoacrylate glue — unless the container is sealed tight, the glue may harden in storage.

Most adhesives are sensitive to surface contaminants, such as wax, oil, silicone, solvents, and dust. If the wood surface is contaminated with wax, for example, water-based glues won't spread properly. Hot-melt glue may break down when it comes in contact with linseed oil, mineral spirits, and other volatile finishing solvents. Contact cement is an incredible dust magnet until it dries, capturing any sawdust that settles on it. This, in turn, weakens the glue joint.

Choose a glue that will work well in your shop environment. Or if you can't match the glue to the shop, adjust the shop to fit the glue. Turn up the heat or the air-conditioning, add a dehumidifier, or thoroughly clean the assembly area.

What wood or wood product will you use? Not all woods, plywoods, and particleboards are equally *bondable*. Some are easier to glue than others. Bondability depends on many factors, but two are particularly important:

■ *Extractives* — These are the oils and minerals that become imbedded in the cell walls of the heartwood, giving a species its characteristic color. Oils prevent glue from penetrating the wood surface and may keep water-based glue from spreading properly. If the extractives are too acidic, they may prevent some glues from curing properly. In rare cases, extractives may react chemically with certain glues.

If you are working with a wood that's difficult to glue, you may wish to test several adhesives to see if one holds better than another. (*SEE FIGURE 1-11.*) Or you can adjust your gluing procedure. Glue up the wood *soon* after you surface it or cut the joinery. Glue

1-11 If you need to compare several different glues, here is a simple test you can do in your own shop using a vise, a hammer, and some wood scraps from the same wood species. Cut the scraps into small blocks all the same size. Using a different glue for each pair of blocks, glue them together face-to-face with the ends overlapping about 2 inches. Let the glue joints cure thoroughly, then mount each pair of blocks in a vise as shown. Strike the uppermost block with a hammer until the joint breaks. Inspect the broken joint — if there was a good glue bond, the wood will break before the glue does and the fibers will be torn from one block or the other. If the bond was weak, it will break along the glue line and there will be few torn fibers.

will not easily penetrate the surfaces of some species of wood, particularly those with large amounts of oily extractives, if the surfaces have been exposed to air for several days. (*SEE FIGURE 1-12.*) You can also screw the clamps a little tighter or use more clamps — the extra clamping pressure will help the glue penetrate the dense wood.

If you're working with oily woods — particularly tropical woods such as rosewood, teak, or ebony — you might also wipe the wood with acetone or naphtha and let it evaporate just before you apply the glue. This will remove some of the oils near the surface and

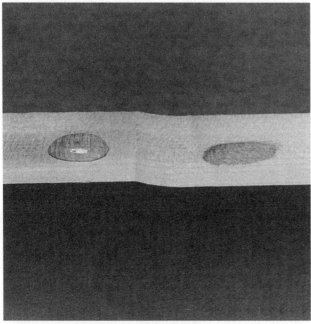

1-12 The surfaces of some woods become case-hardened when exposed to air for several days. (This is not to be confused with hardening from improper drying in a kiln.) This prevents the glue from easily *wetting* the surfaces — that is, it won't penetrate or spread properly. The edge of this piece of yellow pine was jointed and allowed to stand for one week. Afterward, a small portion of the edge near the end of the board was jointed again. Two drops of water were placed on the edge, one on the freshly cut surface and the other on the surface that had been cut a week earlier. After standing for 30 seconds, the drop on the freshly cut surface soaked in and spread out much farther than the other.

allow the glue to penetrate farther. Or you can use glues that are specially formulated for oily woods, such as T-88 and G-2 brand epoxies.

■ *Wood density* — The denser the wood or wood product, the more difficult it is to bond. If the wood is dense, the glue cannot easily penetrate the surface and form an interphase. There are exceptions to this rule — some light woods are as difficult to glue as dense ones — but it's a good guideline. Wood density is measured by its *specific gravity* — the ratio of the dry weight of a volume of wood to an equal volume of water. The higher the specific gravity, the denser the wood. Woods with a specific gravity above .7 are often extremely difficult to glue, and without special glues or gluing techniques, the bonds may be too weak to be reliable. Refer to the chart "Wood Bondability" on the facing page to see the relationship between density and bondability.

How will you use the completed project? There are two important factors to consider:
■ How strong do the wood joints have to be?
■ Will the project be subjected to moisture or high humidity?

Glues are rated for these factors. In fact, glues are rated by the U.S. Forest Products Laboratory (USFPL) for all the properties that determine their durability. Strong glues that resist stress for long periods of time without creeping are classified as "structural"; weaker glues are "semistructural" or "nonstructural." Glues that stand up to moisture, heat, and common chemicals are "exterior"; those that don't are "limited exterior" or "interior." The USFPL uses five classifications:
■ Structural/Exterior
■ Structural/Limited Exterior
■ Structural/Interior
■ Semistructural/Limited Exterior
■ Nonstructural/Interior

Choose the glue with a rating that best describes how the project will be used.

WHERE TO FIND IT

If you need additional information on glue properties, refer to the *Wood Handbook*. This is published by the U.S. Department of Agriculture, Forest Service, and is available at most libraries or from the Government Printing Office (GPO). Write to:

Superintendent of Documents
U.S. Government Printing Office
Washington, DC 20402

WOOD BONDABILITY

WOOD SPECIES	SPECIFIC GRAVITY*	EXTRACTIVES†	BONDABILITY
Alder, red	.41	Medium	Good
Ash, white	.60	Low	Satisfactory
Basswood	.37	Low	Good
Beech	.64	Low	Poor
Birch	.60	Medium	Poor
Butternut	.38	Medium	Good
Cedar, aromatic	.37	High	Good
Cedar, western	.32	High	Excellent
Cherry, black	.50	Medium	Satisfactory
Chestnut	.43	Medium	Excellent
Cypress	.46	Low	Excellent
Ebony	.91	High	Poor
Elm	.50	Low	Good
Fir	.37	Medium	Excellent
Hemlock	.42	Medium	Good
Hickory	.72	Low	Poor
Larch	.52	Medium	Excellent
Mahogany	.45	High	Good
Maple, hard	.63	Low	Poor
Maple, soft	.48	Low	Satisfactory
Oak, red	.63	Medium	Satisfactory
Oak, white	.67	Low	Satisfactory
Pecan	.66	High	Satisfactory
Pine, white	.35	Medium	Good
Pine, yellow	.41	High	Good
Poplar, yellow	.42	Low	Excellent
Redwood	.35	High	Excellent
Rosewood	1.00	High	Poor
Spruce	.37	Medium	Excellent
Sycamore	.49	Medium	Satisfactory
Teak	.55	High	Poor
Tupelo	.50	Medium	Good
Walnut	.55	High	Satisfactory
Willow, black	.39	Low	Excellent

*When dried to 12 percent moisture content
†Relative concentrations

PROPERTIES OF COMMON ADHESIVES

TYPE	CLASSIFI-CATION	APPLICATIONS	GAP FILLING	SANDA-BILITY	COST
Cooked Hide Glue	Nonstructural/ Interior	General interior woodworking; antique restoration; veneering; joinery that can be easily disassembled	Fair	Good	Moderate
Liquid Hide Glue	Nonstructural/ Interior	General interior woodworking; complex assemblies requiring long open time; joinery that can be easily disassembled	Fair	Good	Economical
Polyvinyl Resin (White) Glue	Nonstructural/ Interior	General interior woodworking	Fair	Poor	Economical
Interior Aliphatic Resin (Yellow) Glue	Nonstructural/ Interior	General interior woodworking; gluing oily woods	Fair	Fair	Economical
Exterior Aliphatic Resin (Yellow) Glue	Semistructural/ Limited Exterior	General interior woodworking; gluing oily woods; kitchen and bathroom projects; outdoor furniture	Fair	Fair	Economical
Urea-Formaldehyde (Plastic Resin) Glue	Structural/ Limited Exterior	General woodworking; veneering; complex assemblies requiring long open time; architectural structures; bent laminations	Poor	Good	Moderate to expensive, depending on brand
Cyanoacrylate (Super) Glue	Nonstructural/ Interior	Small repairs; bonding nonporous materials to wood; securing inlays	Poor to fair, depending on formula	Fair	Expensive
Quick-Set Epoxy Cement	Semistructural/ Limited Exterior	Bathroom and kitchen projects; gluing oily woods; bonding nonporous materials to wood; repairs	Good	Good	Expensive
Slow-Set Epoxy Cement	Structural/ Exterior	Bathroom and kitchen projects; gluing oily woods; outdoor furniture; architectural structures; boat building; bonding nonporous materials to wood; securing inlays; bent laminations	Good	Good	Moderate to expensive, depending on quantity bought
Resorcinol Glue	Structural/ Exterior	Bathroom and kitchen projects; outdoor furniture; architectural structures; boat building; bent laminations; complex assemblies requiring long open time	Good	Good	Expensive
Mastics	Semistructural/ Limited Exterior	Securing plywood, wallboard, or foam to framing lumber, masonry, or concrete; non-load-bearing architectural structures	Excellent	Poor	Economical
Silicone Caulk	Nonstructural/ Interior	Bonding nonporous materials to wood	Good	Poor	Moderate
Contact Cement	Nonstructural/ Interior	Veneering; bonding plastic laminates to wood or wood products	Poor	Poor	Moderate to expensive, depending on quantity bought
Hot-Melt Glue	Nonstructural/ Interior	Simple projects; small repairs; temporary assemblies; joinery that can be easily disassembled	Excellent	Poor	Economical

WORKING TEMPERATURES (F)	CRITICAL TIMES				COMMENTS/CAUTIONS
	SHELF LIFE/ POT LIFE	OPEN ASSEMBLY TIME	CLOSED ASSEMBLY TIME	CURE TIME	
70°–100°, glue must be 125°–140°	Indefinite unmixed/ 1 day mixed	3–5 minutes	2 hours	12–16 hours	Develops tack almost immediately; nontoxic; don't heat glue above 160°F; clean up with water
70°–90°	1 year	15–30 minutes	12–16 hours	1 day	Low toxicity; clean up with water
60°–90°	Indefinite unopened, 1 year opened	5–10 minutes	1 hour	1 day	Nontoxic; freezing ruins uncured glue; clean up with water
45°–110°	18–24 months	5–10 minutes	30 minutes	1 day	Develops tack in about 1 minute; low toxicity; freezing ruins uncured glue; clean up with water
45°–110°	1 year	4–8 minutes	25–30 minutes	1 day	Critical times are slightly faster than interior formula; develops tack in about 1 minute; freezing ruins uncured glue; clean up with water
70°–100°	1 year unmixed/ 3–5 hours mixed	10–20 minutes	12–14 hours	1 day	Uncured glue is toxic to skin; cured glue dust (from sanding) is toxic when inhaled, so use adequate ventilation and protection; clean up with water
65°–180°	Varies with formula	15–30 seconds	1 minute	2–4 hours	Despite its interior classification, it is water-resistant; will bond skin, so use acetone to dissolve bonds; vapors can irritate nose and eyes and may cause headaches, so use with adequate ventilation
35°–200°, depending on formula	Indefinite unmixed/ 5 minutes mixed	1–5 minutes	5 minutes	12–24 hours	No clamping pressure required; uncured glue is toxic and may cause allergic reactions, so use adequate ventilation and protection; resists moisture and chemicals, but not heat — most formulas soften at 160°F; clean up with vinegar
35°–200°, depending on formula	Indefinite unmixed/ 1 hour mixed	30–60 minutes	2–4 hours	12–24 hours	No clamping pressure required; uncured glue is toxic and may cause allergic reactions, so use adequate ventilation and protection; resists moisture and chemicals, but not heat — most formulas soften at 160°F; clean up with vinegar
70°–110°	1 year unmixed/ 3 hours mixed	15–30 minutes	10–14 hours	1 day	Strongest of all glues; uncured glue is toxic to skin; cured glue dust (from sanding) is toxic when inhaled, so use adequate ventilation and protection; clean up with water
65°–110°	Indefinite unopened	5–10 minutes	2–4 hours	1 day	May irritate skin, nose, and eyes, so use adequate ventilation and protection; clean up with mineral spirits
65°–180°	Indefinite unopened	10–15 minutes	2–4 hours	1 day	Despite its interior classification, it is waterproof; may irritate skin, nose, and eyes, so use adequate ventilation and protection; clean up with mineral spirits
65°–180°	1 year	15–30 minutes	Bonds on contact	1 day	Vapors are highly toxic; solvent-based formulas are very flammable, so use adequate ventilation; clean up with acetone
32°–160°	Indefinite	5–10 seconds	30–60 seconds	1 minute	Glue may break down when exposed to some finishing chemicals; tip of glue gun is extremely hot, so be careful not to touch it

2

CLAMPING

Although a well-made glue joint eventually becomes stronger than the surrounding wood, it doesn't do so immediately. Most glue joints have little strength until the glue begins to cure. While the glue is still liquid, it cannot hold the wooden parts together on its own — you'll probably rely on one or more *clamps* to press the pieces together for a short time while the bond develops.

There are dozens, perhaps hundreds, of kinds of clamps. General-purpose clamps, such as hand screws and bar clamps, are intended to hold together many sizes and shapes of wooden parts, in as many arrangements as possible. Others, such as frame clamps and edge clamps, have just a few special applications. The types of clamps you need will depend on what you have to clamp up.

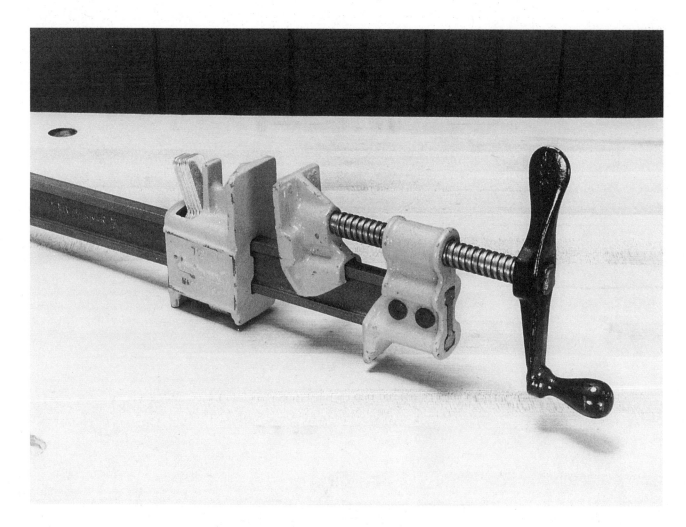

USING CLAMPS

There are three reasons to clamp boards together as you glue them up. First, unless the project is extremely simple, you'll want to *test fit* the parts temporarily before final assembly — that is, assemble them without glue to make sure the joints fit properly. (Some woodworkers refer to this as *dry assembly.*) This task usually requires clamps to hold the parts together dry.

After you apply glue, the wooden parts must remain properly aligned while it dries. Very few glues bond so quickly that you can simply press the parts together in your hands for a short time. The only exceptions are contact cement, which bonds immediately; cyanoacrylate glue, which bonds in one minute; and quick-set epoxy cement, which bonds in five minutes.

Finally, most glues require pressure to bond properly. The pressure helps the glue penetrate the wood and form interphases. Clamps bring the gluing surfaces into intimate contact with one another, squeezing air from the joint and reducing the glue into a thin, even line. The thinner the glue line, the stronger the joint. Remember, when the wood is properly bonded, the glue lines are no thicker than a piece of paper.

FOR YOUR INFORMATION

The single exception to these clamping rules is epoxy cement. Epoxy does *not* need clamping pressure to bond properly. Furthermore, epoxy is so cohesive that thick glue lines are actually stronger than thin ones. Some craftsmen even build up *fillets* of epoxy around a joint to buttress the parts.

The amount of pressure required varies with the wood density. Light softwoods require between 100 and 150 pounds of pressure per square inch (psi). Domestic hardwoods need between 150 and 250 psi, and extremely dense, imported tropical woods may require as much as 300 psi. Different clamps deliver different amounts of pressure. A traditional hand screw, for example, produces between 800 and 1,000 pounds. A bar clamp produces as much as 2,000 pounds, a large C-clamp produces a little over 1,000 pounds, and a medium-size spring clamp produces only about 25 pounds.

But specific gluing pressures are not all that important in day-to-day woodworking. You rarely need to calculate the pressure to get a good bond because an extremely wide range will work for any given glue joint. What is important is that the pressure be *relatively even* all along the glue joint. (*SEE FIGURES 2-1 AND 2-2.*) Remember, a glue line must be uniform in thickness for maximum strength, and to achieve this, it must cure under uniform pressure. To apply uniform pressure, simply space the clamps evenly along the joint. Most glue manufacturers recommend placing clamps every 6 to 12 inches.

You *can,* however, apply too much or too little pressure. If you're working with softwoods and using bar clamps or C-clamps that generate heavy loads, you can crush the wood fibers if you screw them down too tight. It's very difficult to crush the wood fibers of hardwoods with the types of clamps that are normally found in a small shop, but you might choose the wrong clamps and not generate enough pressure. If there's too little pressure, the adhesive will not spread out completely and the glue line will be thick and uneven. Or the glue may not penetrate the wood surface. In both cases, the joint will be weak and may fail.

FOR YOUR INFORMATION

You cannot cause a *starved joint* — a glue joint with too little glue in it — by applying too much pressure. The glue will be absorbed into the wood before too much can be squeezed out of the joint. The only way you can starve a joint is by applying too little glue in the first place.

As you apply the pressure, make sure the wood parts remain properly aligned. Unless the clamps are aligned perfectly perpendicular to the glue joint when

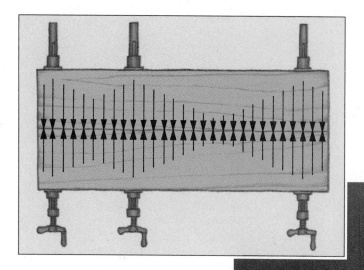

2-1 To generate even pressure
along a glue joint, space the clamps
evenly, taking care that you don't
space them too far apart. The pressure generated by each clamp is
greatest directly under the jaws and
falls off as you go out from the jaws.
If the clamps are too far apart, the
pressure between them may be insuf-
ficient to develop a good glue bond.

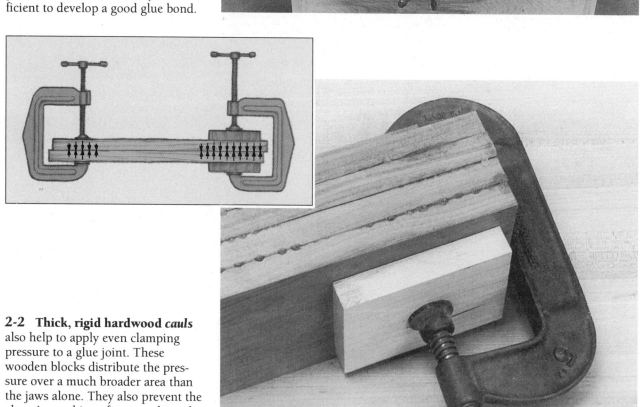

2-2 Thick, rigid hardwood *cauls*
also help to apply even clamping
pressure to a glue joint. These
wooden blocks distribute the pressure over a much broader area than
the jaws alone. They also prevent the
clamp's metal jaws from crushing the
wood fibers directly beneath them.

you tighten them, they will exert a small amount of pressure *sideways*. This may cause the parts to shift slightly while the glue is still liquid. If you've glued up several small wooden blocks face-to-face, you know how frustrating it can be to keep them all aligned as you tighten the clamps — they slide every which way. There are several ways you can avoid this frustration:

■ If you must fasten several parts together, glue one surface at a time. Keeping two parts aligned as you tighten the clamps is a great deal easier than keeping three or more in place.

■ Hold the parts together in your hands for several minutes until the glue develops sufficient tack to keep the parts from shifting. Then apply the clamps carefully, tightening them just enough to keep them in place. When you've positioned all the clamps, screw them down one at a time until each is tight.

■ Use hot-melt or cyanoacrylate glue to prevent the parts from shifting. Or sprinkle the glue surface with a granular substance such as abrasive grit to stop the parts from sliding easily. (*See Figures 2-3 and 2-4.*)

2-3 To keep parts from shifting out of alignment when you glue them together, apply a liquid adhesive to the entire gluing surface except one small area in the center. Apply a small amount of hot-melt or cyanoacrylate glue to this area, then immediately press the wooden parts together and align them. Wait for the quick-setting glues to harden — this takes just a few seconds for hot-melt adhesive, but may require up to a minute for cyanoacrylate — then apply the clamps. **Note:** Hot-melt glue typically spreads out to a thickness of .010 to .015 inch — somewhat thicker than the optimum for most liquid glues. Therefore, the glue bond in the *immediate* vicinity of the hot-melt adhesive will be slightly weaker than elsewhere. This is not a problem with cyanoacrylate glue.

2-4 Or you can keep parts from shifting with a granular substance. Rub two sheets of 50-grit sandpaper together to remove some of the abrasive grit, sprinkling a *small* amount of this abrasive on the wet glue. Press the parts together with enough force to imbed the grit into the surfaces of both boards. **Note:** You can also use sugar or salt, but these may dissolve in water-based glues before you get the boards together.

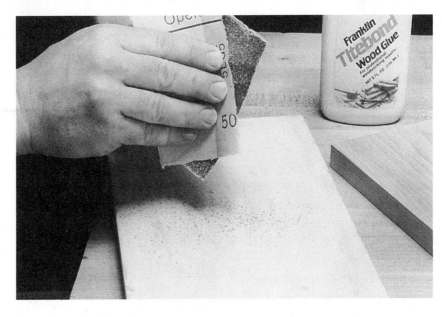

CHOOSING CLAMPS

Because there are so many clamps, they can't all be discussed here. We'll just touch on the more commonly used clamps and clamping fixtures.

TYPES OF CLAMPS

Hand screws are one of the oldest types of clamps in common use today. Their advantages are that they have a deep reach, or *throat,* and that the wooden jaws will not mar the work surface. *(SEE FIGURE 2-5.)* Contemporary hand screws have advantages over traditional ones:

■ *Traditional hand screws* consist of two wooden screws and two parallel wooden jaws. One screw adjusts the opening of the jaws, while the second screw tightens the jaws on the work.

■ Most contemporary hand screws are *swivel-nut hand screws*. These look similar to traditional hand screws, but they have metal screws and operate very differently. Both screws can be used independently to adjust and tighten the jaws. Furthermore, the threaded nuts through which the screws run are able to pivot about 30 degrees. This makes it possible to adjust the angle of the jaws to match the work.

TRY THIS TRICK

When applying a hand screw directly over a glue joint, place a piece of wax paper or plastic wrap between the joint and the wooden jaw of the clamp. Otherwise, you may glue the clamp to the project!

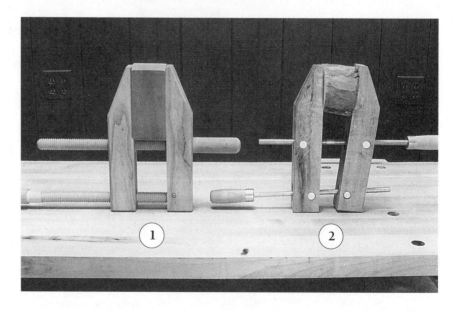

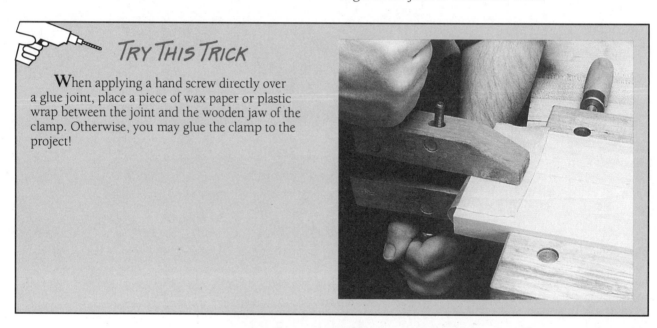

2-5 *Traditional hand screws* **(1)** must be used with the jaws parallel to one another, while the jaws of *swivel-nut hand screws* **(2)** can be angled up to 30 degrees.

While hand screws have a deep throat, **bar clamps** have a wide jaw opening, or *capacity*. This opening is determined by the length of the bar — the longer the bar, the greater the capacity. Most bar clamps have one stationary jaw, usually attached to an end of the bar, and one adjustable jaw that slides back and forth along the bar to adjust the capacity. One of these jaws is fitted with a screw so the clamp can be tightened. Bar clamps differ in the type of bar they employ *(SEE FIGURE 2-6)*:

■ The most common (and the least expensive) bar clamp is a *pipe clamp*. These are cast-iron fittings for standard ½- and ¾-inch-diameter plumbing pipe. (The pipe must be threaded on one end to attach the fitting with the movable jaw.) Some craftsmen keep pipes from 2 to 6 feet long on hand, then attach the clamp fixtures to pipes of the appropriate length for whatever work they're gluing up. There are also special fittings available to extend the throat of common pipe clamps. *(SEE FIGURE 2-7.)*

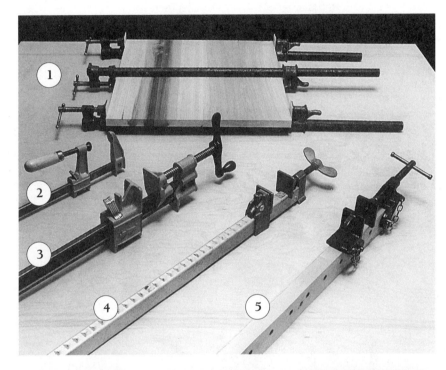

2-6 Bar clamps are distinguished by their type of bar. The most common are *pipe clamps* (1), cast-iron fittings that mount on plumbing pipe. Other choices include *flat bar clamps* (2), iron *I-beam clamps* (3), aluminum *U-beam clamps* (4), and fittings to make *wooden bar clamps* (5).

2-7 *Jaw extenders* fit over standard ¾-inch pipe clamp fittings to increase the throat capacity. These extenders are available from most mail-order woodworking suppliers.

■ *Flat bar clamps* have a longer reach than most, but the bars are not as rigid and so the capacity is limited to a few feet.

■ *Beam clamps* are the most rigid of all bar clamps. There are several shapes of beams available — I-beams, T-beams, and U-beams. Both I-beam and T-beam clamps are usually made from iron and are quite heavy. The beams of U-beam clamps are made from aluminum, and, although they aren't as rigid as iron beam clamps, they are much lighter.

■ *Wooden bar clamps* are cast-iron fittings that can be attached to lengths of wood. They are designed to fit 1-inch-thick lumber, and you can cut the wooden bars however long you need.

In addition to these general-purpose bar clamps, there are also several bar clamps designed for specific tasks (*SEE FIGURE 2-8*):

■ *Reversible pipe clamps* will exert pressure out from the ends of the bar as well as in toward the middle. This makes them useful for taking assemblies apart as well as for clamping them together.

■ *Double bar clamps* are used with a pipe on each side of the work. This keeps the pipes from flexing and bowing under heavy pressure. Consequently, you can apply a lot of pressure, and the work will remain flat and true.

■ *Four-way clamps* are similar to double bar clamps and are used with a wooden bar on each side of the work. However, both the jaws and the bars exert pressure. The work is squeezed from four directions and remains absolutely flat.

■ *Cam clamps* are light-duty flat bar clamps that are operated by throwing a lever or cam. The pressure can be applied very quickly since it take less time to

2-8 Special-purpose bar clamps are designed for specific tasks. For example, a *four-way clamp* (1) presses in from all four sides. A *double bar clamp* (2) exerts pressure without bowing, and a *reversible pipe clamp* (3) pries assemblies apart as well as squeezes them together. A *cam clamp* (4) is designed for small projects and light duty, while a *quick-action bar clamp* (5) can be applied with one hand.

flip a lever than it does to turn a screw. However, these don't exert as much pressure as other bar clamps and are best suited to small projects.

■ *Quick-action bar clamps* are also light-duty flat bar clamps, but they can be applied with one hand by squeezing a lever.

C-clamps come in all shapes and sizes. The body of a C-clamp is a frame with one open side. The jaws — one fixed, one adjustable — are attached to the open side. Compared to hand screws and bar clamps, C-clamps have a small throat *and* a limited capacity. However, they are less bulky than other clamps and easier to apply to small assemblies or in tight spaces. They are also less expensive, so you can afford more of them. There are just three types of C-clamps (*SEE FIGURE 2-9*):

■ Ordinary *C-clamps* are shaped like an oval or a rectangle and have more capacity than throat.

■ *Deep-throat C-clamps* have more reach than other C-clamps, although just how much reach depends on their design. On most deep-throat C-clamps, the throat is approximately equal to the capacity. But on others, the throat is greater.

■ On *quick-action C-clamps,* the jaws are extensions of locking pliers. Adjust the opening, then lock the jaws closed by squeezing the handle of the pliers together.

Edge clamps and *cross clamps* apply pressure from three directions (*SEE FIGURE 2-10*):

■ Most *edge clamps* look like C-clamps with three adjustable jaws instead of one. Two of the screws are

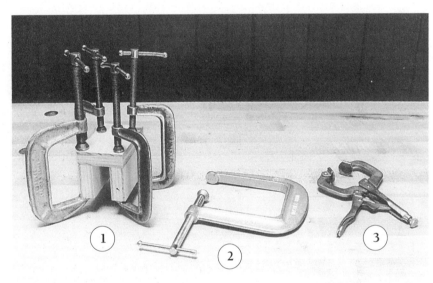

2-9 **Because *C-clamps* (1) have a** small throat and capacity, they are best suited for small projects and assemblies. If you need slightly more reach than an ordinary C-clamp will provide, use a *deep-throat C-clamp* (2). *Quick-action C-clamps* (3) hold the work in the same manner as locking pliers.

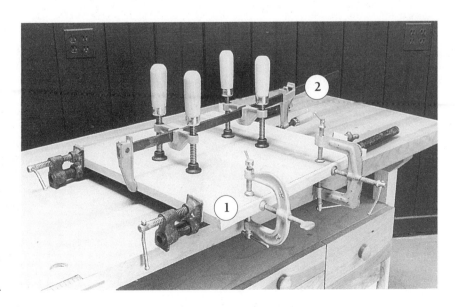

2-10 *Edge clamps* (1) look like C-clamps with an extra jaw and are used to apply edging or banding to a workpiece. *Cross clamps* (2) are used to clamp edging, and they can apply pressure to the middle of a wide panel.

parallel to and aligned with one another, while the other is perpendicular to the first two. Use the two parallel screws to secure the clamp to the workpiece, then tighten the perpendicular screw to exert pressure against an end or an edge.

■ *Cross clamps* are designed to work with flat bar clamps. They hook onto the bar, and two screws exert pressure perpendicular to the clamp jaws. In addition to clamping pieces to the end or edge of a board, cross clamps can also apply pressure to the middle of a wide panel.

Band clamps are flexible bands that wrap around a workpiece and constrict it. They are used for clamping frames, cylinders, boxes — any assembly that encloses a space. Often used for trial assembly, there are two basic types (*SEE FIGURE 2-11*):

■ Ordinary *ratchet-action band clamps* are made from long cloth tape, the ends of which are attached to a ratchet mechanism. As the ratchet winds up the bands, they tighten around the workpiece.

■ *Elastic band clamps* are simply long strips of rubber that wind around an assembly. As you wind them, stretch them slightly so they squeeze the work.

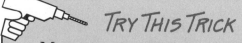

TRY THIS TRICK

Make your own elastic band clamps from strips of rubber tire inner tube or surgical tubing.

Miter clamps hold frame and box parts square to one another. You can use them to assemble one corner of the frame or box at a time or all the corners at once (*SEE FIGURE 2-12*):

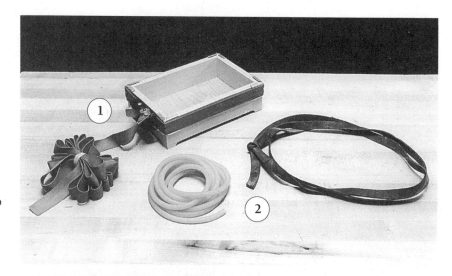

2-11   Ratchet-action band clamps (1) are made from cloth tape that loops around the assembly. This loop is tightened with a ratchet. *Elastic band clamps* (2) are strips of rubber that stretch around a project and tighten when the rubber constricts.

2-12   Corner clamps (1) are designed to help assemble a single 90-degree corner. They are sometimes used along with other clamps to hold an assembly square while the glue dries. *Frame clamps* (2) hold all four members of a four-sided frame together.

■ *Corner clamps* hold two pieces of wood square to one another. While they are ordinarily used to assemble the miter joints of frames, they can also be used to hold the parts of drawers and boxes. This helps keep these assemblies perfectly square.

■ *Frame clamps* hold all the parts of a frame in alignment, enabling you to assemble all the corner joints at once. Normally, these specialized fixtures hold only four-sided assemblies. To hold hexagonal, octagonal, and other odd-shaped frames, you must either use band clamps or make your own special frame clamps.

Hold-downs clamp the work to the surface of a workbench or secure it in a fixture (*SEE FIGURE 2-13*):

■ The shaft of a *holdfast* fits in a hole in the workbench, while its arm extends over the work. When you whack the top of the shaft with a hammer, it sticks deeper in the hole, and the spring tension in the arm presses the work against the bench.

■ A *screw holdfast* looks similar to an ordinary holdfast, but you turn a screw to put tension on the arm. This, in turn, clamps the work to the bench.

■ *Toggle clamps* are miniature lever-activated hold-downs. When you throw the lever, the arm presses down. Toggle clamps are often used to make special-purpose clamping jigs.

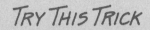

TRY THIS TRICK

In a pinch, you can use the quill of a drill press as a hold-down. Fully retract the jaws inside the chuck and place the assembly you want to clamp under the quill. Advance the quill feed until the chuck presses the work down on the drill press table, then secure the quill lock.

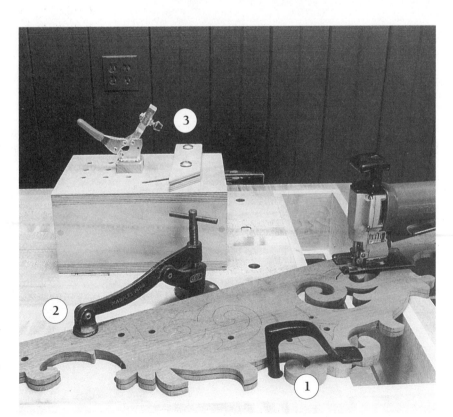

2-13 A traditional *holdfast* (1) clamps the work to the workbench by spring tension, while a *screw holdfast* (2) uses a screw to generate clamping pressure. *Toggle clamps* (3) are miniature holdfasts that you can use to make clamping fixtures and other jigs.

Presses are usually designed for face-to-face glue-ups and exert pressure over a broad area (*SEE FIGURE 2-14*):

■ A *veneer press* positions several powerful press screws over a broad work surface. Rigid iron cauls distribute the pressure from these screws, so you can clamp thin sheets of veneer to broad panels.

■ A *bending press* or *lamination press* clamps together thin layers (laminations) of wood between two broad jaws. The surfaces of these jaws are often curved and lined with pneumatic tubes to distribute the pressure evenly. The craftsman cuts the laminate stock extremely thin to make it flexible enough to conform to the curves when clamped in the press. Once the glue between the layers has dried, the laminated assembly holds the curve.

Finally, a *spring clamp* works like a large clothespin. The jaws are held closed by a large spring. (*SEE FIGURE 2-15*.) Of all the clamps listed, these generate the least clamping pressure. However, they are extremely quick to apply and are often used to hold work together temporarily until more substantial clamps can be applied.

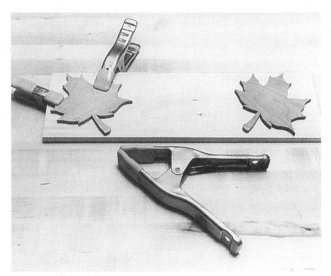

2-15 Like oversize clothespins, *spring clamps* generate clamping pressure with springs. Although you cannot adjust this pressure as with other clamps, you can increase it by adding more clamps to the workpiece.

2-14 A *veneer press* (1) uses several press screws and iron cauls to distribute clamping pressure over a broad area. A *bending press* (2) clamps thin, flexible pieces of wood together face-to-face between curved jaws. After the glue has dried, the assembly retains these curves.

CLAMPING HARDWARE AND MATERIALS

In addition to clamps, there are many different types of hardware that will hold wood together. For example, nails and screws are actually small clamps that can be installed permanently to help glue up assemblies that would be difficult to hold together with external clamps.

There are other fasteners that are used as clamps. *Pinch dogs,* for example, are U-shaped nails that straddle a joint. (*SEE FIGURE 2-16.*) When driven partway into the wood, they squeeze the parts together. After the glue has dried, the dogs are removed and if necessary, the small holes they leave are filled.

Various workshop and household materials can also serve as clamps. Masking tape makes a good light-duty clamp for some operations. So does rope: You can tighten a length of rope around an assembly like a tourniquet. Or make wedges from scraps of wood and use them in place of edge clamps and cross clamps. Some craftsmen even keep a few bags of lead shot around their shops to weigh down projects that can't be clamped. (*SEE FIGURES 2-17 THROUGH 2-20.*)

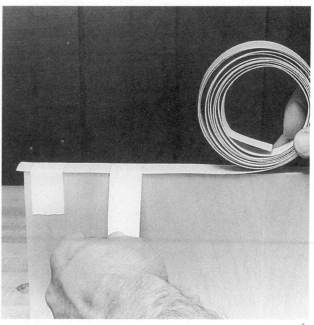

2-16 Pinch dogs are reusable U-shaped nails designed to hold two boards together temporarily. Place each pinch dog to straddle the joint between the boards, then hammer the dogs partway into the wood. The pointed ends are inclined so that the deeper you drive the dogs, the tighter they draw the joint. When you need to remove the dogs, grasp the protruding end with pliers and pull.

2-17 Because masking tape is slightly elastic, you can use it as a light-duty clamp. Simply stick it to the wood, stretching it over the joint. Here, multiple pieces of tape are used to clamp veneer banding to the edge of a plywood board.

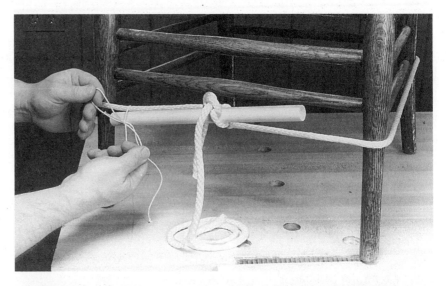

2-18 You can make a serviceable band clamp from a length of rope. Wrap the rope around the assembly and tie the ends together, making a loose loop. Place a stick under the knot inside the loop, and use it to twist the rope. As you continue to twist, the loop will tighten. When the loop is as tight as you want it, tie one end of the stick to the rope to prevent it from unwinding.

2-19 You can use *wooden wedges* to exert clamping pressure, provided you can brace them against something. Here, several wedges were driven under a bar clamp and a C-clamp. The bar clamp wedges keep the wood panel from bowing, while the wedge under the C-clamp keeps the boards aligned. You might also use wedges with C-clamps when applying edging and banding.

2-20 Weights also make good clamps, and one of the most useful clamping weights is a 25-pound bag of lead shot. Like bean bags, these bags conform to the shape of the wooden parts that you want to weigh down — there's no need to balance them. You can purchase lead shot from stores that sell firearms or hunting supplies.

CAULS

The metal jaws of commercial clamps can mar the wood surface. Clamping pressure is the most intense immediately under the jaws. This crushes the wood fibers, leaving small dents or depressions in the wood. To protect the wood, you must insert *cauls* between the clamp jaws and the wood surface. You can make these cauls from many different materials.

Note: In addition to protecting the surface, large, thick cauls also distribute the clamping pressure, as noted earlier. Small wooden cauls and cauls made from flexible materials such as rubber or plastic do *not* distribute the pressure; they are only protective.

1 **One of the best (and the** least expensive) materials to use for cauls is scrap wood. You might want to keep a container full of small, thin pieces of wood on hand to place under clamp jaws. When you need to distribute clamping pressure over a broad surface, use larger, thicker scraps. **Note:** If you find it difficult to keep the wooden cauls in place as you apply the clamps, stick the wood cauls to the wood surface with double-faced carpet tape.

2 **Wood biscuits (for plate** joinery) also make good cauls. You can keep a container of biscuits handy or glue them permanently to the clamp jaws with epoxy cement.

(continued) ▷

CAULS — CONTINUED

3 **In addition to wood, you can** use thick pieces of leather, rubber, and plastic as cauls. Several woodworking suppliers sell sheets of plastic with an adhesive backing for this purpose. Cut the plastic to size and shape with tin snips, peel off the protective paper, and stick the plastic to the clamp jaw.

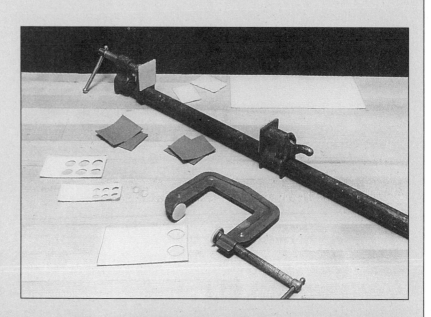

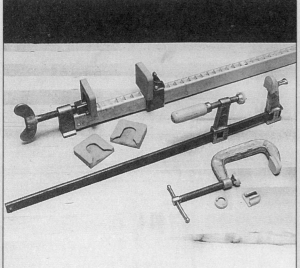

4 **Some woodworking suppliers** also sell molded rubber pads that fit the jaws of bar clamps and C-clamps. The advantage of these fitted rubber cauls is that they can be easily removed should you need to use the clamp without cauls.

5 **Perhaps the most versatile** caul material is a sheet of flexible magnetic plastic glued to a flat block of wood. Using scissors, cut the magnetic material and glue it to the wood with epoxy cement. Since most commercial clamps are made from iron, the cauls will stick wherever you place them. If you need to use the clamp without cauls, simply remove them.

CLAMP HANGERS

Not only do you need a variety of clamps, you also need places to store them. These wall-mounted clamp hangers are designed to hold the four most common types of clamps — hand screws, band clamps, bar clamps, and C-clamps. They are simple to build and easy to use — they hold the clamps so that they can be quickly retrieved when you need them.

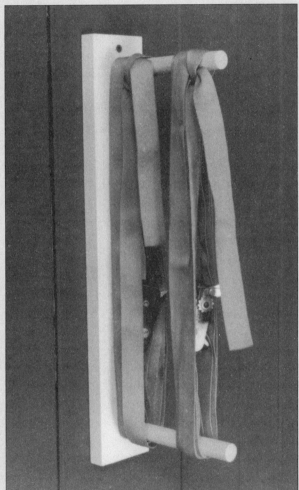

1 **This rack stores hand screws** in a vertical stack. Use the adjustable shelves to separate different sizes. To stack a hand screw, adjust the jaws so they are open 1½ inches or wider, then slide the screw onto the appropriate shelf or place it on top of the appropriate stack. When you need a hand screw, simply slide the size needed out of the stack.

2 **Rolling and unrolling a band** clamp when taking it in and out of storage is a nuisance. This simple hanger eliminates the chore. Simply loop a clamp around the two pegs, pull it snug, then wind up the excess band. The hanger can be mounted to the wall horizontally or vertically.

(continued) ▷

CLAMP HANGERS — CONTINUED

3 **These brackets store bar** clamps of all different lengths horizontally. Use two brackets, spaced about 20 inches apart, to store 2- and 3-foot-long clamps. Mount a third bracket so all three are spaced 20 inches on center to hold 4-, 5-, and 6-foot-long clamps.

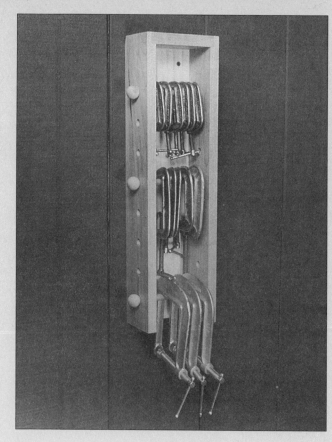

4 **This boxlike storage unit** holds small and medium-size C-clamps — just hook the C-clamps over the dowels. Adjust the level of the hanger dowels so a stored C-clamp won't bang against the hanger below it.

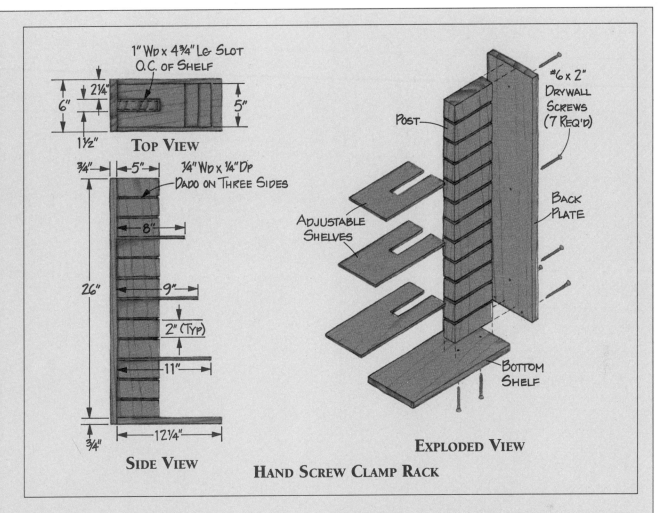

1" Wd x 4¾" Lg Slot O.C. of Shelf

2¼"
6"
5"
1½"

TOP VIEW

¾"
5"
¼" Wd x ¼" Dp Dado on Three Sides

8"
26"
9"
2" (Typ)
11"

¾"
12¼"

SIDE VIEW

POST
ADJUSTABLE SHELVES

#6 x 2" DRYWALL SCREWS (7 REQ'D)

BACK PLATE

BOTTOM SHELF

EXPLODED VIEW

HAND SCREW CLAMP RACK

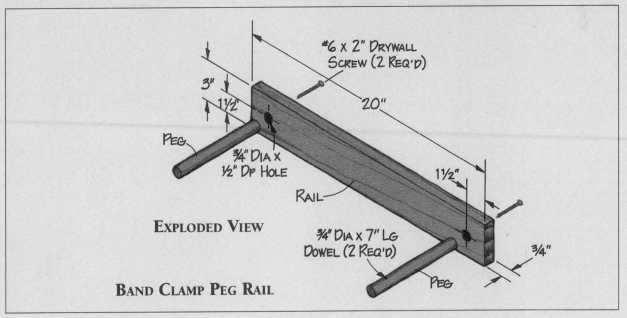

#6 x 2" DRYWALL SCREW (2 REQ'D)

3"
1½"
20"

PEG
¾" DIA x ½" DP HOLE

RAIL

1½"

¾"

EXPLODED VIEW

¾" DIA x 7" LG DOWEL (2 REQ'D)

PEG

BAND CLAMP PEG RAIL

(continued) ▷

CLAMP HANGERS — CONTINUED

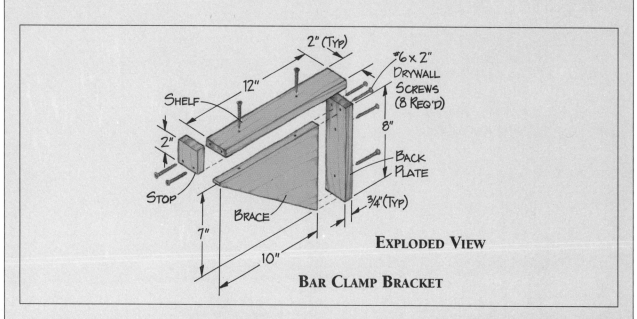

2" (TYP)

12"

SHELF

#6 x 2"
DRYWALL
SCREWS
(8 REQ'D)

8"

2"

BACK
PLATE

STOP

BRACE

3/4" (TYP)

7"

10"

EXPLODED VIEW

BAR CLAMP BRACKET

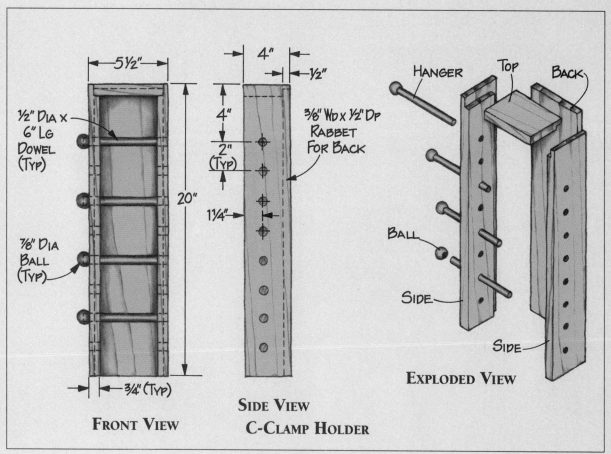

5½"

½" DIA x
6" LG
DOWEL
(TYP)

20"

⅞" DIA
BALL
(TYP)

3/4" (TYP)

FRONT VIEW

4"

½"

4"

2"
(TYP)

1¼"

⅜" WD x ½" DP
RABBET
FOR BACK

SIDE VIEW
C-CLAMP HOLDER

HANGER

TOP

BACK

BALL

SIDE

SIDE

EXPLODED VIEW

3

BASIC GLUING TECHNIQUES

Once you have selected the proper glue and clamps for the job, all that's left to do is spread some glue on the wood and clamp the parts together, right? Well, not quite. There's more know-how required for even the most basic gluing procedures than you might think.

The wood parts that you wish to glue together must be properly prepared for gluing — and so should you! The stock should be dry and relatively stable. There must be enough gluing surface in the joint to create a strong bond, and this surface must be clean and smooth. You must be sure that the parts fit together easily and that you can assemble them within the glue's allotted open assembly time.

When mixing and spreading the glue, you should take pre- cautions to protect yourself — some glues contain hazardous chemicals. After applying the glue, clean up any excess material that has squeezed out of the joint. Finally, allow the assembly to remain in the clamps long enough for a strong bond to develop; then, if the joint is to be sanded or machined, wait an additional period for the glue to cure to full strength.

PREPARING THE WOOD

SHOP DRYING

To get a strong glue bond, the wood must be properly dried and relatively stable *in your shop environment.* If there is too much moisture in the wood, it will weaken a glue joint. That's because as the wood dries and releases the excess moisture, it shrinks. This shrinkage causes the parts to fit poorly, stresses the glue joint, and may even break the joint.

To reduce the moisture and control the movement, the lumber should be either air-dried or kiln-dried before you build anything with it. If you're using an exterior glue (such as epoxy or resorcinol), the wood must be dried to a moisture content of 10 to 14 percent. For interior glues, such as white or yellow glue, the optimum moisture content will range from 6 to 11 percent, depending on the average relative humidity in your area. *(SEE FIGURE 3-1.)*

Don't think that just because the wood is air-dried or kiln-dried that you can use it immediately. It must also be conditioned to your shop. That is, the boards must be allowed to rest in your shop for several weeks before you use them so their moisture content will adjust to the relative humidity of the room. This is referred to as *shop drying,* although, in some cases the boards may actually take on additional moisture. Whether the moisture content increases or decreases, this conditioning *is extremely important!* Even though the wood may be dried to the recommended moisture content for your area, it must be allowed to acclimate itself to the specific environment in which it will be worked. Otherwise, the wood may move after you cut and assemble the parts of your project, ruining it.

Failure to properly shop-dry wood before working it is one of the most common — and most costly — errors of novice and experienced craftsmen alike. To emphasize how essential this step is, let me tell you about a small chest of drawers I once made. I brought the stock home from the kiln and cut and assembled the parts of the case that same day. The next day I made the drawers. Several days later I returned to apply the finish, but by then the wood was in motion. The case, which was originally 9 inches deep, had shrunk to $8\frac{7}{8}$ inches so the drawers protruded $\frac{1}{8}$ inch! The drawer construction would not allow me to shorten the drawers, and I had to remake them completely — but only after I let the case shop-dry for a few weeks to make sure it wouldn't shrink any further.

FOR YOUR INFORMATION

Some craftsmen forgo shop-drying, then try to control the wood movement by applying a finish as quickly as possible. This is only a partial solution at best. All common wood finishes are *semipermeable* — although they slow the release and the absorption of moisture, they don't stop it completely. Eventually, the moisture content reaches an equilibrium with its environment and, as it does, the wood moves.

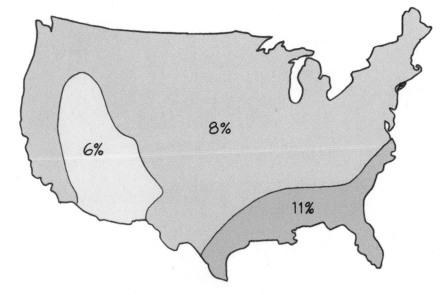

3-1 After wood has dried sufficiently, the *average* moisture content will stabilize. It may continue to go up or down with changes in the seasons — and the wood will move accordingly — but it will hover around a certain percentage. This percentage is determined by the prevailing relative humidity of the area. In the humid regions of the southeastern United States, the moisture content will stabilize at approximately 11 percent. In the arid western deserts, it will reach as low as 6 percent. Throughout most of the country, however, the average is 8 percent.

ORIENTING THE WOOD GRAIN

The strength of the glue joint also depends on how you orient the wood grain of the adjoining parts — certain arrangements create stronger bonds and minimize the effects of wood movement better than others. (*SEE FIGURE 3-2.*) There are four possible orientations:

■ Long grain to long grain with the grain parallel, as when gluing boards edge to edge

■ Long grain to long grain with the grain perpendicular, as when gluing a mortise-and-tenon joint

■ Long grain to end grain, as when gluing a shelf in a dado

■ End grain to end grain, as when joining the mitered members of a frame

The strongest and most durable glue joints have long grain parallel to long grain. Wood is fairly stable along the wood grain but expands and contracts across it. As long as the wood grain is aligned so the parts expand and contract the same amount and in the same direction, this movement will not affect the joint. Joints that are glued long grain to long grain with the grain perpendicular may be strong, but because the adjoining surfaces expand and contract in different directions, the joint is stressed. If there is too much stress, the assembly may warp or twist, and

the joints will eventually break. To prevent this, follow a simple rule of thumb: *When the wood grain directions are perpendicular, the gluing surfaces shouldn't be any wider than 3 inches across the grain. (SEE FIGURE 3-3.)* If one or both of the surfaces are too wide, there are several remedies:

■ Cut large surfaces into smaller ones. Although wide boards were available, old-time craftsmen made the backs of cabinets from narrow ones for just this reason. It's easier to accommodate the movement of several narrow boards than one wide one.

■ Use *floating* joints to capture a wide part and hold it in place without glue. In frame-and-panel construction, for example, the panel floats in grooves. There is enough clearance between the edges of the panel and the bottom of the grooves to allow the panel to move freely without stressing the glue joints that hold the frame together.

■ Use fasteners instead of glue. Finishing nails bend slightly as the wood moves, yet they continue to hold. You can use screws in the same manner if you drill slots or oversize holes for the screw shanks.

Joints that are glued long grain to end grain are weaker than those with long grain only, and end-grain-

3-2 Much of the strength and durability of a glue joint depends on the way in which the wood grain of adjoining members is oriented. The strongest, most durable glue joint you can make is to join the wood *long grain to long grain with the grain parallel* as you do when gluing boards edge to edge (1). Next is long grain to long grain with the grain perpendicular as they are in a mortise-and-tenon joint (2). This is just as strong as a joint with long grain parallel to long grain, but not as durable since the cheeks of the tenon expand and contract in a different direction than the sides of the mortise. *Long-grain-to-end-grain* joints, such as a typical dado joint (3), may be just as durable as some long-grain-only joints, but they are not as strong. End grain absorbs a great deal more glue than long grain, partially starving the joint and making it weaker. For this same reason, *end-grain-to-end-grain* joints, such as miter joints (4), are the weakest of all.

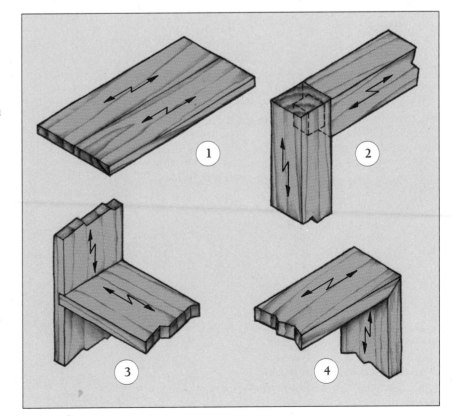

to-end-grain joints are weaker yet. This is because too much glue penetrates the wood and the joint is starved. However, you can increase the strength of these joints by sealing the end grain before assembling the parts. Apply a thin coat of glue to the end-grain surface and wait 10 to 20 minutes. Then apply more glue and clamp the parts together. The first application of glue partially hardens and prevents the wood from absorbing the second application.

In addition to grain direction, you must also consider the orientation of the annual rings. Not only does wood expand and contract across the grain but it also moves twice as much *tangentially* to the annual rings as it does radially. *(SEE FIGURE 3-4.)* For the best possible glue joint with the least amount of stress, you should align the radial and tangential planes as closely as possible.

For example, you should not glue plain-sawn lumber face-to-face with quarter-sawn lumber. *(SEE FIGURE 3-5.)* Plain-sawn lumber is sliced tangent to the annual rings, while quarter-sawn lumber is cut radially. Consequently, the two types of boards expand and contract at different rates — even when they are the same species! If you glue them together, the joint will be stressed. This consideration applies to all kinds of joints, not just simple face-to-face laminations. *(SEE FIGURES 3-6 AND 3-7.)*

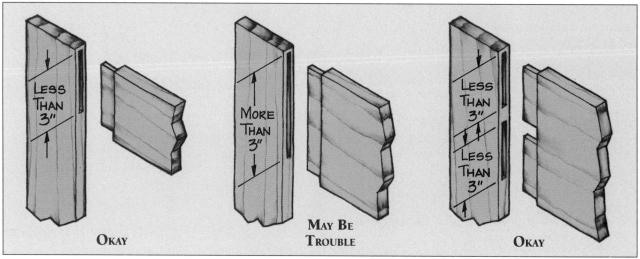

3-3 When gluing long grain to long grain with the grain perpendicular, the gluing surfaces shouldn't be any wider than 3 inches across the grain. Otherwise, the wood movement may overstress the glue joint, causing the parts to warp or the bond to break. For this reason,

you should avoid making mortise-and-tenon joints in which the mortises are too deep or the tenons are too wide. For example, instead of making a joint with a single wide tenon, split it into two or more smaller tenons, each less than 3 inches wide.

3-4 Wood moves approximately twice as much *tangentially* to the annual rings as *radially*. Consequently, if you cut a 2-inch-square board from green (wet) lumber as shown and let it dry, it will shrink to a rectangular shape. Depending on the wood species, the tangential plane will lose about 8 percent of its breadth, while the radial plane will lose only 4 percent.

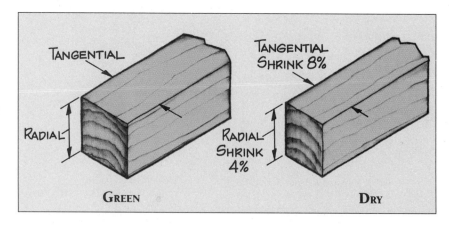

3-5 Plain-sawn lumber is cut *tangent* to the annual rings in the wood, while quarter-sawn lumber is cut radially. Consequently, the two types of lumber move at different rates. If you glue them together face-to-face during dry weather, the assembly is likely to cup toward the quarter-sawn side when the days are humid because quarter-sawn stock expands less than the plain-sawn wood.

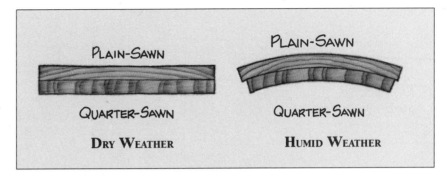

3-6 If the annual rings of adjoining boards aren't properly aligned, the uneven movement may stress the glue joint. For example, a plain-sawn board will shrink and expand more than the quarter-sawn board in which it is held. Both adjoining boards should be either plain-sawn or quarter-sawn.

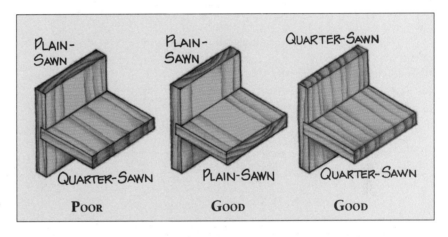

3-7 Aligning the annual rings requires more thought as the joinery grows more complex. Carefully consider the stresses that might develop in a joint to determine the best possible arrangement. When assembling mortise-and-tenon joints, for instance, align the radial surfaces parallel to the depth of the mortise and the width of the tenon. This will keep the wood movement to a minimum where the wood grain directions are perpendicular to one another.

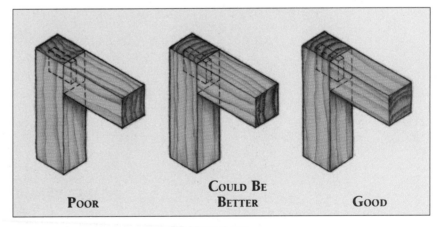

PREPARING THE GLUING SURFACE

One of the most important factors affecting the strength of a glue joint is the surface area. The greater the contact area, the stronger the joint will be. Consequently, you should choose joinery to provide the maximum gluing surface area. Specifically, you want as much long-grain-to-long-grain contact as you can get.

The quality of the gluing surface is just as important as its quantity. The wood surface should be:

■ Smooth, flat, and true, so the gluing areas contact one another all along the joint

■ Without chips or tears, since these will break the continuity of the glue line

■ Free of fuzzy "whiskers" and raised grain, which interfere with the evenness of the glue line

■ Without burnished or crushed fibers, since these prevent the glue from penetrating the wood and forming the vital interphases

■ Free of chemical contaminants, since these may react with the wood or prevent the glue from spreading evenly or penetrating properly

Smooth, knife-cut surfaces make the best glue joints. Wood cut with a planer, jointer, or router will glue up well, provided the mill marks left by the cutters are not deep. Some high-quality saw blades, such as hollow-ground planer blades and precision carbide-tipped blades, cut smoothly. There are also special *abrasive* saw blades designed to leave smooth surfaces that will create a good glue joint. However, ordinary circular saw blades, band saws, jig saws, and hand saws do not. The rule of thumb is that a gluing surface should be *at least* as smooth as a surface sanded with 50-grit sandpaper. The smoother, the better. (SEE FIGURE 3-8.)

To help prepare the surfaces for gluing, make slow, even cuts. The more cuts per inch, the smoother the surface will be. Make sure the joints fit properly — snug but not tight. See that the wood surfaces that are supposed to contact one another actually do. Gaps will keep the glue from squeezing out to a thin, even line.

TRY THIS TRICK

Use a piece of typing paper folded once to test the fit of a joint. When you cover one of the mating surfaces with a double thickness of paper, the joint should be too tight to assemble without force. But when you remove the paper, the parts should slide together easily.

Do the gluing as soon after the cutting as you can — the same day, if possible. Otherwise, the wood surface starts to collect dust, dirt, oils, waxes, and other contaminants. It may also shrink or swell, ruining the fit

of the joint. Remember, some naturally oily woods such as yellow pine and teak become case-hardened when exposed to the air for very long, and their bond-ability decreases. It's especially important to glue up these woods as soon as you can after cutting them.

TRY THIS TRICK

If the wood sits for a long time after the joint is cut, *lightly* sand the gluing surfaces with a fine-grit paper. This will clean the surfaces and expose fresh wood.

GLUING UP

PREPARATION AND PRECAUTIONS

As you glue the parts together, keep an eye on the clock — and the calendar. You must keep track of four different time frames:

- Shelf life or pot life of the glue
- Open assembly time
- Closed assembly time
- Cure time

First, verify that the glue's shelf life has not expired. Since most manufacturers err on the side of caution when estimating a glue's life span, you can sometimes get away with using out-of-date glues. But why take the chance? If the glue doesn't bond, you'll have to scrape it or sand it from all the surfaces before you can apply fresh glue. Oftentimes, you must remake some or all of the adjoining parts.

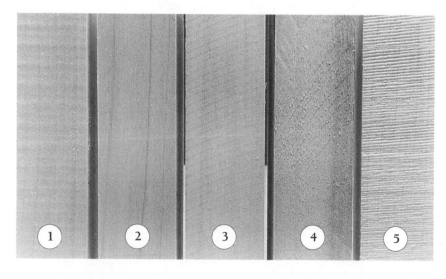

3-8 A planed or jointed surface (1) makes a strong glue joint. So does a routed surface (2). If you sand the surface (3), do so to 50-grit or finer. A surface cut with an ordinary saw blade (4) may not be smooth enough, while one cut with a band saw (5) is almost certainly too coarse.

TRY THIS TRICK

Because most glue manufacturers don't stamp the expiration date on their products, write the purchase date on a piece of tape and stick it on the glue container to help keep track of the shelf life.

If necessary, mix the glue and prepare it for application. Carefully read the labels and any Material Safety Data Sheets that are supplied with the adhesive. Many glues contain toxins, irritants, and flammable chemicals that require you to take precautions.

If the glue is *toxic,* you must not ingest the glue or breathe the vapors. Don't eat or drink in the shop while using it. Wear rubber gloves, especially if you have open cuts on your hands. Open a window or two and use window fans to help ventilate the shop.

If the glue is a possible *irritant,* wear rubber gloves when handling it. When you must handle it for long periods of time, also wear a face shield and cover any exposed skin with petroleum jelly or barrier cream. Refrain from touching your face or other parts of your body until you have cleaned up.

If the glue is *flammable,* ventilate the shop. Don't use the glue if there are any open flames nearby, such as the pilot lights of a furnace or water heater. And don't smoke while using the glue. When working with the glue for long periods, wear a respirator with cartridges designed to remove *organic solvents* from the air you breathe.

Note: Refer to "Properties of Common Adhesives" on page 14 if you are unsure whether or not a specific glue is dangerous.

OPEN ASSEMBLY

Apply the glue in thin, even coats, using a brush, roller, wood scrap, or some other tool to spread it. Pipe cleaners are good tools for coating the sides of holes and slots. (*SEE FIGURE 3-9.*) Fingers make handy glue spreaders on larger areas, of course, provided you don't mind the mess and the glue contains no toxins or irritants. However, it's a better idea to keep some cheap brushes and rollers on hand. (*SEE FIGURES 3-10 AND 3-11.*)

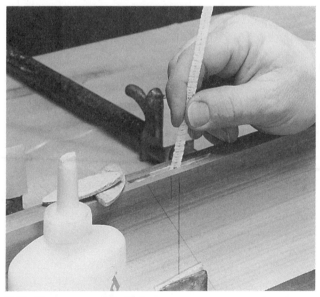

3-9 Keep a supply of pipe cleaners on hand to spread glue in hard-to-reach areas such as dowel holes, spline grooves, and biscuit slots.

3-10 Acid brushes make good applicators for spreading glue over small surfaces. They cost just pennies apiece if purchased in quantity, so you can afford to dispose of them after the glue hardens. If you use water-based adhesives, such as white or yellow glue, clean the used brushes with water. This will dissolve the glue and keep the bristles soft, allowing you to use the brushes over and over.

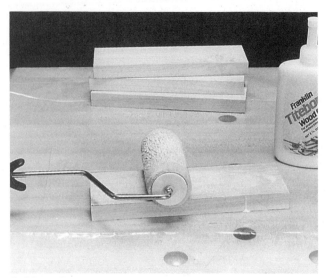

3-11 When you must apply glue to broad areas, use a small paint roller. Purchase inexpensive, disposable rollers with a short nap. You can save money by buying full-size rollers, then cutting them in thirds or quarters.

TRY THIS TRICK

If you want to spread the glue precisely, use a ³/₈-inch-diameter metal rod with fine (24 pitch) threads. Researchers at Franklin International of Columbus, Ohio, have found that when you draw this threaded rod slowly over white or yellow glue, it spreads the adhesive to a uniform depth of .008 inches!

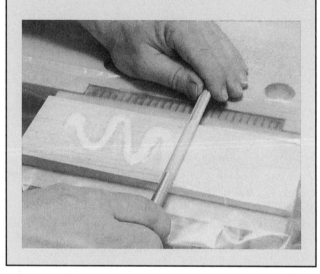

FOR YOUR INFORMATION

There are many ingenious-looking glue bottles with special nozzles or applicators on the market. I have tested many of these, but have yet to find a glue bottle that won't clog when used daily in the shop. When this happens, complex nozzles require more time to clean than simple ones. If you consider this cleaning time, a simple squeeze bottle and an acid brush are a good deal less trouble (and less expensive) than the fancy applicators.

Just how thick or thin should you spread the glue? This depends on the wood species and the type of glue, but manufacturers have found that, in general, glue should be spread .007 to .008 inch thick — about as thick as four sheets of typing paper. When you put the parts together and apply the clamps, some of this glue penetrates the wood to form the interphases, some remains as the glue line, and the remainder squeezes out of the joint. However, don't worry about the precise thickness of the glue coat — for any given gluing operation, there is a wide range of thicknesses that will produce a strong bond. It's much more important that the coat be uniform and even.

CLOSED ASSEMBLY

As soon as possible after spreading the glue, assemble the parts and *apply pressure* with clamps. (Remember, all glues, with the exception of epoxy cement, contact cement, and cyanoacrylate, require prolonged clamping pressure to form a strong bond.) Leave the assembly in the clamps long enough for the glue bond to develop sufficient strength to hold the parts together. This will take anywhere from a few minutes to several hours, depending on the type of glue.

While you're waiting, you may want to clean up the excess glue that oozes from the joint or the *squeeze-out*. Craftsmen disagree on how long you should wait before cleaning up the squeeze-out. Some would have you wipe it off immediately, since it's easier to remove before it dries. Others advise you to wait until the glue hardens, then remove it with a scraper, chisel, or sandpaper. They argue that if you try to wipe off the glue while it's still wet, you could force it deeper into the wood. This, in turn, prevents stains and finishes from penetrating the wood, making light spots or *glue stains* in the finish. (*SEE FIGURE 3-12.*) In fact, glue stains can be a problem, but only if you don't carefully clean up all the excess glue.

How and when you clean up the excess glue really depends on what kind of glue you use and how accessible the squeeze-out is. If you use a water-based glue and you can easily reach the surfaces around the joint, then scrape away most of the squeeze-out with a plastic scraper, and remove any remaining glue by wiping the wood surfaces with a sopping wet rag. (*SEE FIGURES 3-13 AND 3-14.*) The water raises the wood grain, of course, but it can be sanded smooth easily. And in most cases, you must sand the wood after assembly anyway to prepare the surface for a finish.

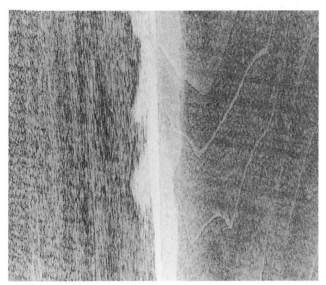

3-12 If you don't carefully clean up the excess glue after assembling a joint, it may contaminate the surrounding surface. It will seal the wood, preventing stains and finishes from penetrating. These glue-contaminated surfaces, or *glue stains,* will remain much lighter than the surrounding wood after you apply a finish.

3-13 After assembling a joint with a water-based glue, clean up the wet squeeze-out with a plastic scraper. (An old credit card makes an excellent glue scraper; the soft plastic won't damage the surface of the wood.) You may have to remove the clamps one at a time to reach all the surfaces around the glue joint.

3-14 After scraping up as much excess glue as possible, thoroughly wash the wood surface with a *sopping* wet rag — don't just wipe it with a damp one. You must use enough water to dissolve any remaining glue and float it away from the surface. After cleaning up the glue, wipe off the excess water. **Note:** For just this purpose, many craftsmen keep a "glue rag" in a small plastic pan partially filled with water.

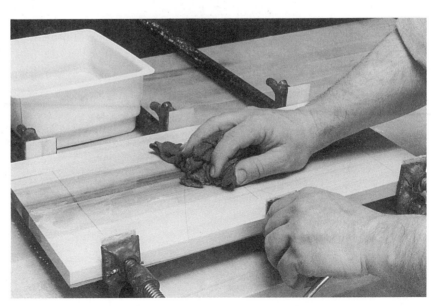

FOR YOUR INFORMATION

There is a misconception that washing away the squeeze-out with water will dissolve or dilute the glue *in the joint* and weaken it. This is not true. When the water contacts the wood surfaces around the joint, they swell up and seal the glue line, preventing the water from entering the joint.

If you're using a glue that isn't soluble in water or if you can't reach the surfaces around the assembled joint, then you must wait for the glue to dry. After it has dried, remove as much of the hardened squeeze-out as you can with a chisel or a scraper. Then sand the surface clean. (SEE FIGURE 3-15.)

TRY THIS TRICK

Even though epoxy cement isn't water soluble, you can clean up the squeeze-out with vinegar before the epoxy dries, provided you first scrape off the excess, then scrub the surface thoroughly. Vinegar also cleans epoxy off your skin.

No matter what method you use, there is always some chance that all the glue might not be removed, causing glue stains in the finish. How can you tell when the surfaces are entirely clean? Wait for the glue to cure completely (at least 24 hours), then wipe the surfaces around the joint with water or VM&P naphtha.

(Both of these materials evaporate completely and will not interfere with the finish.) The clean wood darkens, while the glue-contaminated surfaces remain light. If you find any glue stains, wait for the water or naphtha to evaporate and sand the surfaces again.

3-15 If you let the excess glue dry on the wood surface, scrape it off when it hardens. A glue scraper (shown) works best for this chore. **Warning:** Don't plane or joint surfaces with any hard glue beads — always scrape the beads off first. The beads can dull or nick the knives.

TRY THIS TRICK

To protect the wood from glue squeeze-out so you won't have to clean it at all, cover the surfaces around the joint with masking tape prior to final assembly. After the glue sets up, peel off the tape. This technique is especially handy for protecting the inside corners of boxes and other enclosed assemblies.

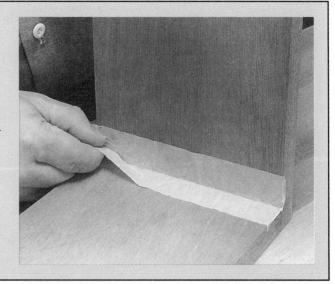

CURING THE GLUE

If you plan to sand or machine the assembly, you must wait for the glue to cure completely. The cure time varies with the glue, but all common glues dry completely within 24 hours.

There are several reasons for waiting. Most important, the joint may come apart if you plane, joint, rout, saw, or otherwise machine the assembly too soon after it comes out of the clamps. This can be very dangerous. The tool might throw the pieces of the assembly at you or anyone who happens to be standing nearby. And if you're feeding the assembly toward the blade or cutter when it comes apart, your hands might slip into the machine. Second, if you plan to sand the assembly, you'll find that the longer the glue cures, the harder it becomes and the easier it is to sand.

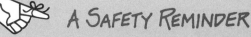

A SAFETY REMINDER

Some glues — particularly plastic-resin glue, resorcinol, and epoxy cement — produce toxic dust when sanded. Wear a dust mask and ventilate the shop when sanding assemblies that have been joined with these adhesives.

If you're using water-based glues, you must allow enough time for the water in the joint to evaporate completely. The water swells the wood, raising the surfaces around the joint slightly. If you sand the joint before the wood dries, you will remove the proud portion of the stock. When the water evaporates, the wood will shrink and the surfaces around the joint will appear sunken. (*SEE FIGURE 3-16.*)

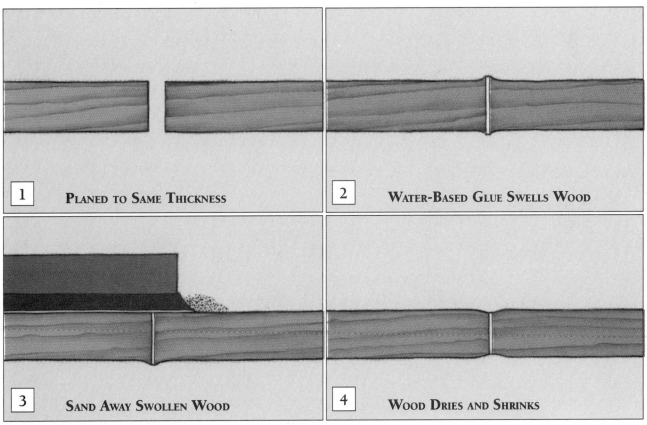

1 PLANED TO SAME THICKNESS

2 WATER-BASED GLUE SWELLS WOOD

3 SAND AWAY SWOLLEN WOOD

4 WOOD DRIES AND SHRINKS

3-16 When joining wood with water-based glues, you must wait for the water to evaporate from the joint before planing, jointing, or sanding the assembly. Initially, the surfaces in a joint are relatively level (1), but the water in the glue swells the wood and raises the surfaces immediately surrounding the joint (2). If you sand these surfaces while they are still wet, you'll remove the high spots (3). When the water evaporates, the wood will shrink and the surfaces surrounding the joint will sink (4).

Common Gluing Problems and Solutions

PROBLEM	POSSIBLE CAUSE	SOLUTION
Weak or failed joints	Not enough gluing surface	Redesign joint or add reinforcement to provide additional surface area.
	Not enough glue (starved joint)	Apply more glue. If gluing end grain, seal ends before gluing up.
	Wood moving in opposite directions	Align wood grain and annual rings so parts move in unison.
	Not enough pressure or uneven pressure	Apply more clamps. Space them evenly along joint.
	Glue line too thick	Apply more clamps. Make sure joint fits properly.
	Gaps and voids in glue line	Spread glue evenly over entire gluing surface. Make sure joint fits properly. If you want glue to fill voids, use epoxy cement or another adhesive with good gap-filling ability.
	Surface too rough	Plane, joint, or rout gluing surfaces if possible. Saw with smooth-cutting blade or sand to at least 50-grit.
	Wrong glue	Choose appropriate glue for particular wood species.
	Wood surface dirty or contaminated	Glue up joint as soon as possible after cutting it. If gluing surface is exposed for several days, lightly sand wood to clean it. If wood is oily, wipe with alcohol or naphtha.
	Shelf life or pot life expired	Purchase or mix fresh batch of glue.
	Assembly required too much time	Choose glue with longer open assembly time, or divide assembly into shorter steps.
	Glue not allowed to cure sufficiently	Leave assembly in clamps for longer period of time; wait for at least 24 hours before sanding or machining.
Creep or steps in joints	Wood moving in opposite directions	Align wood grain and annual rings so parts move in unison.
	Joints are too tight; pressure continues to squeeze hardened glue out of joints	Make sure joints fit properly.
Joints give slightly with time, but don't fail completely	Glue is creeping because of constant stress	Use a glue that is less likely to creep; redesign joinery to better withstand stress.
Sunken joints	Joints are machined or sanded before water from water-based glues can evaporate	Allow water to evaporate completely; wait at least 24 hours before sanding or machining.
Glue stains	Light stain — glue squeeze-out not properly cleaned from surface	If using water-based glue, scrape off excess and wash surface before glue dries. If using other glues, let dry completely, then scrape and sand. Check by wetting surface with water or naphtha.
	Dark stain — iron clamp in contact with joint as glue dried	Make sure pipes and cast-iron parts of clamps do not contact glue joint as glue dries.

4

GLUING UP SIMPLE ASSEMBLIES

Although there are many factors to consider when gluing up a project — wood species, grain orientation, end use, and so on — what usually concerns you the most is how the wooden parts fit together. You must contemplate not just how well they fit, but how the parts are joined and their *geometry* when assembled. This determines the specific assembly procedure that you must use.

There are three basic assembly operations, based on how the parts fit together:

■ Gluing boards *edge to edge* to make wide stock from narrow lumber

■ Gluing boards *face-to-face* (also called *lamination*) to make thick stock from thin lumber

■ Gluing boards *end to end* to make long stock from short lumber

Each operation requires you to apply the glue in a particular manner, assemble the parts in a certain order, and use specific clamps or combinations of clamps.

GLUING EDGE TO EDGE

Craftsmen glue boards edge to edge not only to make wide stock from narrow boards, but for other reasons as well. For example, you can save a cupped or stressed board by ripping it into narrow strips, jointing the edges, and gluing the strips back together again. You can eliminate knots and other defects in the same manner. Or you can create decorative patterns by gluing up strips of different wood species.

Whatever the reason for gluing edge to edge, the assembly procedure is the same. First, joint and plane the boards to a uniform thickness, slightly thicker than the final dimension. (*SEE FIGURE 4-1.*) Cut them a little longer than needed. When laid edge to edge, the assembly should also be a little wider than needed. This extra stock will let you cut, scrape, and sand the assembly to the precise shape and size needed.

Arrange the boards as you want to join them. There are several schools of thought on how you should do this. Some craftsmen cut the strips as wide as possible and orient the annual rings so they all cup up or out. This exposes more of the colorful heartwood to view and, since the heart of the tree is the hardest part, presents the toughest possible surface to resist wear. However, there is a disadvantage to this arrangement. Because the wood tends to cup in the opposite direction of the annual rings, the assembly may raise up or bow out in the center. However, this can be prevented with simple brace work.

Others cut the wood into narrow strips, sometimes only 1 or 2 inches wide, then alternate the direction of the annual rings. This, in fact, is the method most glue manufacturers advise. It creates a much more stable board than the first option, but the glued-up assembly may not look as nice or wear as well. (*SEE FIGURE 4-2.*)

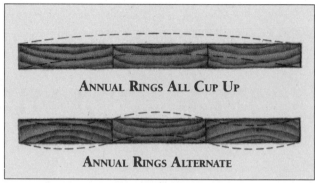

ANNUAL RINGS ALL CUP UP

ANNUAL RINGS ALTERNATE

4-2 There are several conflicting schools of thought as to how you should arrange boards when gluing them edge to edge. Some craftsmen rip wide strips, arranging them so the annual rings all cup up or out. This creates an assembly that looks good and wears well, but is not particularly stable. Others cut the wood into narrow strips and alternate the direction of the annual rings. This is more stable, but not always as aesthetically pleasing. Most opt for aesthetics, provided the wood is stable and free of defects.

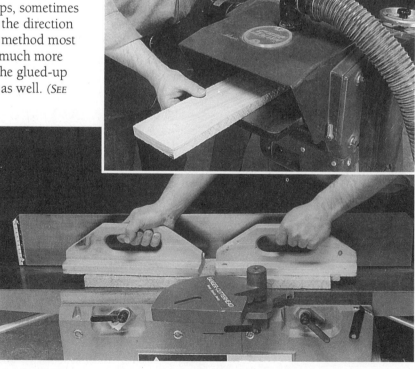

4-1 To prepare lumber before gluing it edge to edge, first *joint* one face of the wood. This will remove any cup or warp. Then *plane* the second face parallel to the first.

However, most craftsmen try not to let these rules stand in the way of common sense. If the lumber is reasonably flat and properly shop-dried, you should arrange the boards so the most attractive sides show and the grain pattern on each piece matches its neighbors.

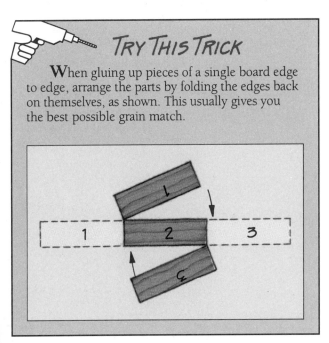

TRY THIS TRICK

When gluing up pieces of a single board edge to edge, arrange the parts by folding the edges back on themselves, as shown. This usually gives you the best possible grain match.

Once you have arranged the boards, mark their faces so you can realign them easily when assembling them. (*SEE FIGURE 4-3.*) Joint the edges you wish to glue together, making them perfectly straight. (*SEE FIGURE 4-4.*)

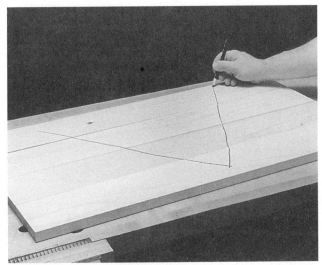

4-3 Once the boards are arranged, use a pencil to make two diagonal marks across them, forming a large "V." These marks will show you which edges to joint and help you to align the parts when it's time to glue them together.

4-4 After marking the wood, joint the edges in the order in which you will assemble them. When jointing the first edge, turn the board so the marks face out. Turn the marks on the second edge to face in; turn them out again for the third, and so on. This technique compensates for any error in the alignment of the jointer fence. Even if the fence is not perfectly square to the table, the boards will fit together correctly. **Note:** Depending on the wood grain, some boards can be jointed in one direction only; if jointed in the wrong direction, they may tear out. When this is the case, you won't be able to use this technique. Just make sure the jointer fence is properly aligned.

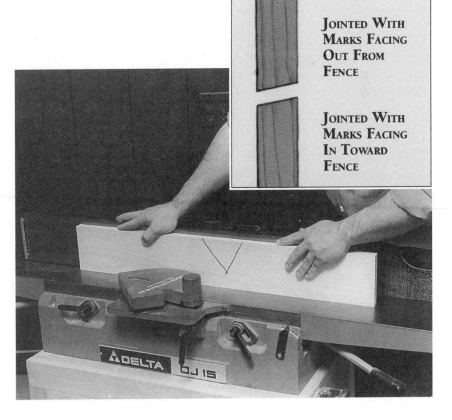

JOINTED WITH MARKS FACING OUT FROM FENCE

JOINTED WITH MARKS FACING IN TOWARD FENCE

FOR YOUR INFORMATION

Some craftsmen joint the edges *slightly* concave (making the depth or *chord* of the curve no more than $1/64$ to $1/32$ inch). When glued up, the boards are pinched together tighter at the ends than in the middle. This procedure supposedly keeps the ends from checking or splitting, but it may have just the opposite effect. The fibers at the ends of the board are crushed and are therefore *more likely to split!* Joint the edges straight. If wood is properly shop-dried and reasonably free of defects, it shouldn't split.

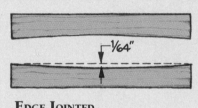

**EDGE JOINTED
SLIGHTLY CONCAVE**

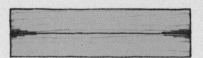

**WHEN BOARDS ARE
ASSEMBLED, WOOD FIBERS
ARE CRUSHED NEAR ENDS**

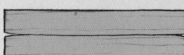

**AFTER SEVERAL HUMIDITY
CYCLES, BOARDS CHECK
NEAR ENDS**

In addition to jointing the edges, you can also cut edge joints to increase the gluing surface and to help align the boards as you glue them together. (*SEE FIGURE 4-5.*) There are several joints that will do the job; the one you pick depends on the tools you have available and your own preferences.

Assemble the boards *without glue,* using bar clamps to hold the assembly together. Alternate the clamps top and bottom — this will help prevent the assembly from buckling. Tighten the clamps and watch for possible problems. Are there gaps between the boards? Do they require excessive pressure to force them together? Does the assembly remain flat? If there are problems, correct them before you apply the glue.

When you're certain that there are no problems with the joinery, loosen the clamps. Set aside the clamps that straddle the *top* surface of the assembly, leaving the bottom clamps where they are. Turn all the boards, except the last one, so one edge faces up. (*SEE FIGURE 4-6.*) Apply the glue to the top edge of the boards you have turned. (The last board needs no glue.) Lay the boards down again in the proper order on the bottom clamps. Align the pencil marks, replace the top clamps, and tighten all the clamps. (*SEE FIGURE 4-7.*)

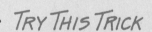

TRY THIS TRICK

If you need longer bar clamps than you have available, make a super-long bar clamp from two shorter ones. Hook the movable jaws of the clamps over one another, as shown. If you're using pipe clamps, join two pieces of pipe with a pipe coupler.

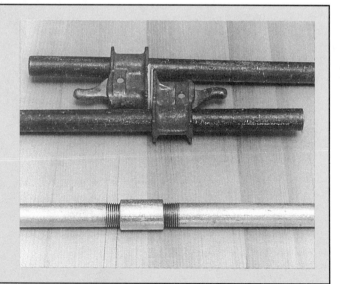

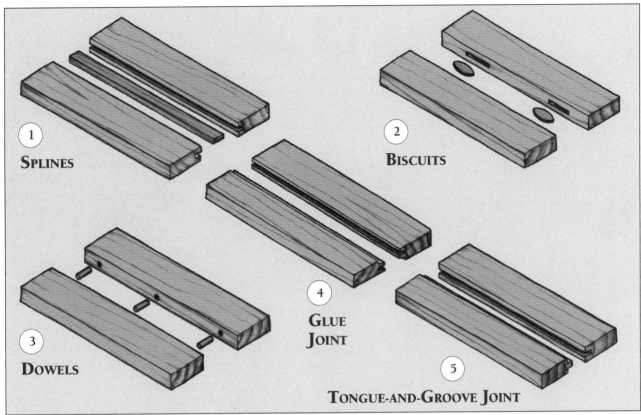

1 SPLINES

2 BISCUITS

4 GLUE JOINT

3 DOWELS

5 TONGUE-AND-GROOVE JOINT

4-5 There are many different edge joints to help align the boards and to strengthen the bonds between them when gluing stock edge to edge. *Splines* (1) are slender strips of wood or plywood that rest in grooves that have been cut in the adjoining edges. *Biscuits* (2) are short, football-shaped splines made from compressed wood. These fit in curved kerfs made with a biscuit joiner (also called a plate joiner). *Dowels* (3) are inserted in holes in the adjoining edges. These holes are precisely positioned with the aid of a doweling jig. *Glue joints* (4) are cut with a special router bit or shaper cutter. Each edge is cut to the same shape, then every other board is turned face for face. *Tongue-and-groove joints* (5) are cut with two matching cutters. One edge is cut with the tongue shape; the other is grooved.

4-6 Adjust the bar clamps and arrange them so you can apply pressure to the assembly as soon as possible after you apply the glue. Place the boards in the order in which you will assemble them, and apply glue to just *one* edge of each board (except the edge of the last board which will become the end). Use a brush to spread the glue evenly over the surfaces.

Use different clamping tools to glue up boards with
beveled edges. If the beveled boards create an enclosure, such as an octagonal box, wrap band clamps
around the assembly. If they make a single corner,
fashion simple jigs from scraps of wood to keep the
boards at the proper angle to one another. Rest the
boards in the jigs, then apply pressure with band
clamps. (*See Figure 4-8.*)

4-7 As you apply the bar clamps
to the assembled boards, space them
evenly *along both faces.* Arrange the
clamps so they alternate between the
top and bottom faces, as shown. This
evens out the pressure on both sides
of the assembly and helps keep it
from buckling. If the boards shift or
slide as you apply pressure and the
top and bottom faces won't remain
flush, use a few C-clamps to straddle
the joints near the ends of the boards,
as shown. Some craftsmen prefer to
wait a few minutes for the glue to
develop some tack, then place a wood
block over the joint (to protect the
work) and smack the block with a
mallet until the joint is flush.

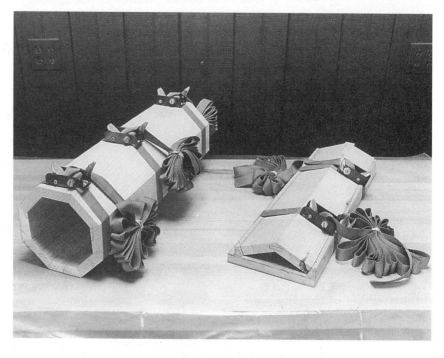

4-8 When the edges of the boards
are beveled, use band clamps to glue
them edge to edge. If the assembly
forms an enclosure, simply wrap
several band clamps around it. If the
beveled boards create a single corner,
make a C-shaped jig, as shown. This
will hold the boards at the proper
angle to one another as you tighten
band clamps around the boards and
the jig.

GLUING FACE-TO-FACE

Face-to-face lamination is used extensively to create large, solid blocks for lathe work or wood carving. Even though the wood grain is aligned in the same direction, this operation is very different from edge-to-edge gluing because you must apply lots of pressure to a much broader area. The best tool for this particular clamping job is a veneer press, which is capable of generating vast amounts of clamping pressure and distributing it over a large surface.

However, there are few small workshops that can boast of having a veneer press. And because most shops have a limited number of clamps, it's sometimes difficult to generate enough pressure for large laminations. Furthermore, since most clamps have a short reach, you may not be able to distribute the pressure evenly.

There are ways around these problems. If you have a small number of clamps, you can supplement them with weights — any heavy object will do. Or if your clamps won't reach the center of a wide gluing surface, stretch long wooden beams across the assembly and fasten them down. (SEE FIGURE 4-9.) Old-time craftsmen braced long poles or *go-bars* between the top of their workbenches and the ceiling of their shops to apply pressure to the middle of broad boards. (SEE FIGURE 4-10.)

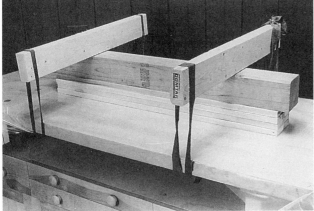

4-9 Here are a couple of inexpensive ways to clamp up large face-to-face laminations without using clamps. You can stack *concrete blocks* on the assembly to generate pressure; if ordinary blocks aren't heavy enough, use *solid* concrete blocks, which weigh over 70 pounds apiece. Or lay lengths of construction lumber across the assembly and fasten them to the workbench with strips of rubber inner tube, as shown. Use broad, thick cauls to help distribute the pressure.

4-10 Old-time craftsmen clamped up broad laminations with *go-bars* — long, supple poles that they braced between their workbenches and the ceiling in their shops. To generate more pressure, they simply used more go-bars.

To prepare the wood, true the faces of the boards with a jointer and a planer — joint the first face, then plane the second face parallel to it. Arrange the boards with their grain parallel, and alternate the direction of the annual rings to keep the assembly from warping. (SEE FIGURE 4-11.)

Arrange the clamps (or whatever clamping apparatus you're using for this operation) and assemble the boards without glue. Then loosen the clamps, set them aside where you can easily reach them, and apply glue to *one* face of each board (except for the last board). Stack the boards together as you apply the glue. After gluing up the last board, quickly apply the clamps.

The boards will probably want to slide or shift out of alignment — shifting is more of a problem with this type of assembly than with any other. The broad boards literally float on the liquid glue and slide sideways the moment you apply pressure. To prevent this, use one of the techniques described in "Using Clamps" on page 17. Or just glue up two or three pieces at a time rather than fight to keep the whole stack aligned.

TRY THIS TRICK

By laminating different species of wood and carefully arranging the boards so that the colors of the adjoining boards contrast, you can produce a decorative effect. This effect is heightened when you cut through the assembly at an angle, making the laminations appear broader. You can also cut a curve in it with a band saw or scroll saw; a simple curve forms ellipses while the results are unpredictable if you cut complex shapes. Finally the contrasting laminations can be turned on a lathe.

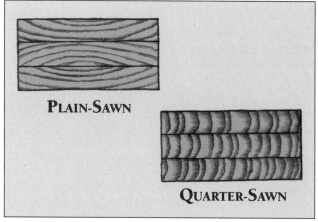

PLAIN-SAWN

QUARTER-SAWN

4-11 When gluing wood face-to-face, alternate the direction of the annual rings of plain-sawn lumber. Since the boards tend to cup in the opposite direction of the annual rings, this will balance the stress and keep the assembly from cupping at all. If you're using quarter-sawn lumber, the orientation of the annual rings isn't important since this wood has little tendency to cup in the first place. However, be careful not to mix the two types of lumber in the same lamination because they expand and contract at different rates.

GLUING END TO END

Gluing wood end to end is more common in construction than in fine woodworking — carpenters often join boards in this manner to create long beams or joists. But as the price of wood continues to go up, furniture makers and hobbyists are doing it more and more. It's an excellent way to use up the short lengths in your scrap bin. The glued-up wood is strong enough for medium- and light-duty applications; if you don't want to see the seams, you can use the glued-up wood for parts that won't be visible on the completed project.

As stated earlier, end-grain-to-end-grain glue joints are the weakest you can make. Consequently, most craftsmen cut the joint to increase the gluing surface (SEE FIGURE 4-12):

■ An *end lap* creates a good deal of long-grain-to-long-grain gluing surface. Furthermore, you can cut the lap as long as you deem necessary to create a strong joint.

■ A *bridle joint* is harder to make than an end lap, but offers twice as much long-grain gluing surface.

■ A *finger joint* is the end joint preferred by most furniture manufacturers and professional craftsmen because it's quick to make. However, it requires a special shaper cutter or router bit. (*SEE FIGURE 4-13.*)

■ A *scarf joint* is the traditional method of joining two boards. A well-made scarf joint is the strongest method of joining two boards end to end, but when poorly done, it's the weakest. (*SEE FIGURE 4-14.*)

Test fit the end joints to check for potential problems, arrange your clamps, and practice the assembly procedure. You'll find that end-to-end gluing operations present two unusual problems. You must keep the surfaces of the boards aligned precisely so the assembly will be straight. And you must devise some way to press the ends of the boards together, which can be difficult if the assembly is very long.

Special L-shaped cauls will solve both these problems. The cauls are long enough to keep the boards aligned, and have cleats affixed to the ends to provide a purchase for the clamps. Use two cauls for each joint. (*SEE FIGURES 4-15 AND 4-16.*)

When the joints fit properly and you have gathered the clamps and other materials needed to assemble them, apply the glue. Remember that end grain joints require more glue than normal since the end grain absorbs more glue. For the strongest possible joint, seal the end grain with a light coat of glue, wait 10 to 20 minutes, then apply more glue and clamp the boards together.

4-13 You must cut finger joints using a special router bit or shaper cutter, available through many mail-order woodworking suppliers. Carefully adjust the depth of cut so you can cut the ends of both adjoining boards precisely the same, then flip one board face for face to join them together.

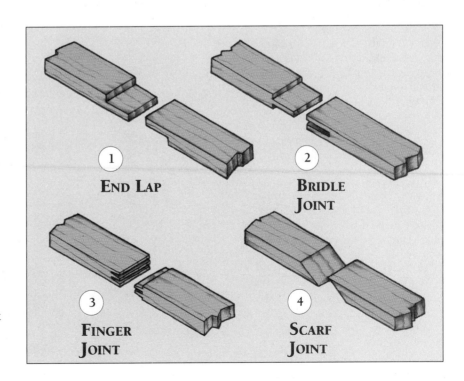

4-12 While there are many end joints to choose from, the four most common are the *end lap* (1), the *bridle joint* (2), the *finger joint* (3), and the *scarf joint* (4).

1 **END LAP**

2 **BRIDLE JOINT**

3 **FINGER JOINT**

4 **SCARF JOINT**

4-14 There are many different types of scarf joints, and many ways to reinforce them. To make a strong scarf joint, you must make an angled cut long enough to provide sufficient gluing surface — traditionally, craftsmen cut scarf joints with slopes of 8 to 1. To make the joint even stronger, you might add *splines* (1) or biscuits to straddle it, fasten the members with *bolts* (2) or pegs, apply *gussets* (3) or plates to the outside surfaces, or even cut angled *mortises and tenons* (4) to add long-grain gluing surfaces.

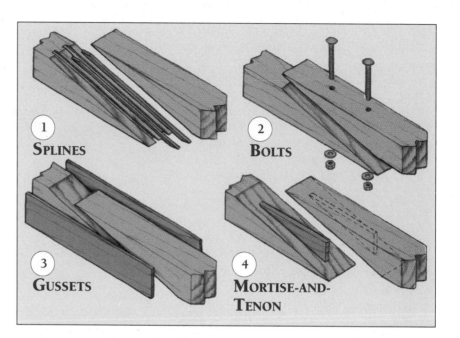

4-15 To glue two boards end to end, first make two long, L-shaped cauls, as shown. Cover the joints with waxed paper to prevent the cauls from sticking, then apply the cauls to cradle the joint. Arrange clamps to straddle both cauls and squeeze the joint together. Tighten the clamps until the joint is snug, but don't tighten them completely.

4-16 Clamp a hand screw to each of the two boards, just a few inches from the ends of the cauls. Tighten these two hand screws as much as you can. Then apply several more hand screws, straddling the first two clamps and the cleats on the ends of the cauls, as shown. These will press the ends of the boards together. When you're sure that there are no gaps between the ends of the boards, completely tighten the clamps that hold the cauls to the boards.

5

GLUING UP COMPLEX ASSEMBLIES

Rarely do craftsmen have the luxury of assembling one type of joint at a time. Usually, they must assemble several pieces, gluing up two or more types of joints at once. And often, the assemblies are large or complex. These complex assemblies present special problems, and there are special gluing procedures for dealing with them.

Although the specific assembly techniques vary widely from project to project, they can be divided into four general types:

■ Gluing up *box assemblies,* as when making drawers or small chests

■ Gluing up *frame-and-panel assemblies,* such as paneled doors and window frames

■ Gluing up *leg-and-rail assemblies,* including tables, chairs, and stools

■ Gluing up *case assemblies,* as when making the case for a chest of drawers or a bookcase

ASSEMBLING BOXES, DRAWERS, AND CHESTS

In a typical box assembly, such as a drawer or a small chest, all four sides of the box have the wood grain aligned horizontally so they expand and contract together. The bottom of the box usually floats in grooves — it is *not* glued. These grooves are cut into the inside surfaces of the ends and sides.

The sides and the ends of the box can be joined with dozens of different joints, from simple butt and miter joints to intricate finger joints and dovetail joints. However, the choice of joinery isn't as important as the geometry of the assembled parts. When gluing up the assembly, you must hold the sides square to one another. Furthermore, the assembly should be flat — it must not rock or tip when you set it on a flat surface.

There are several clamps you can use during assembly, depending on the size of the box and its configuration. Bar clamps and band clamps are the easiest to use for all but the smallest boxes. *(SEE FIGURES 5-1 AND 5-2.)* Bar clamps work best for large boxes or boxes with complex joinery that require plenty of pressure. Band clamps are best used for more delicate assemblies.

5-2 You can also use band clamps to keep a box together. However, these clamps do not generate as much pressure as bar clamps and may not be suitable for large boxes. They are best used for small or light constructions.

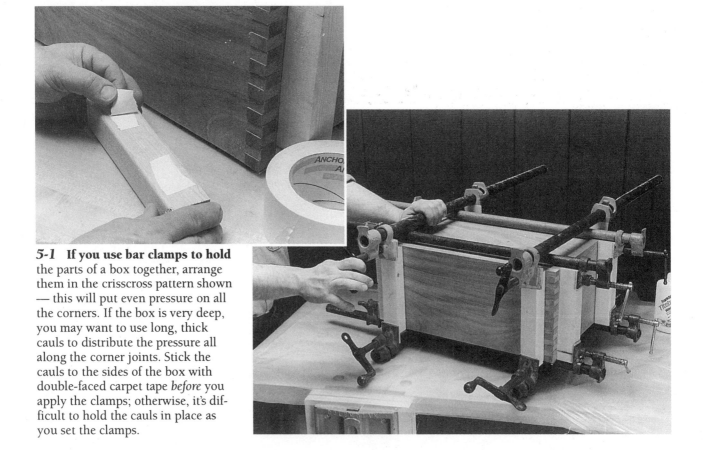

5-1 If you use bar clamps to hold the parts of a box together, arrange them in the crisscross pattern shown — this will put even pressure on all the corners. If the box is very deep, you may want to use long, thick cauls to distribute the pressure all along the corner joints. Stick the cauls to the sides of the box with double-faced carpet tape *before* you apply the clamps; otherwise, it's difficult to hold the cauls in place as you set the clamps.

TRY THIS TRICK

If you join the corners of the box with dovetail joints or finger joints, make special *cogged* cauls, as shown. These apply pressure directly to the individual tails, pins, and fingers.

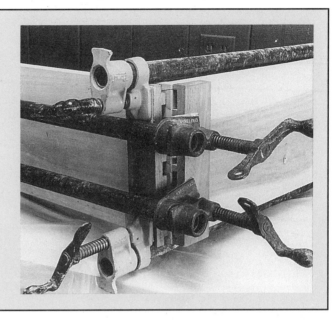

As you glue and clamp the box parts, you must hold the assembly square and flat. To determine if the assembled box is true, you can check the inside corners with a small square. Or measure from corner to corner diagonally. If the lengths of both diagonals are equal, the assembly is square.

If the corners are *not* square, you'll find that two of the corners are *acute* (less than 90 degrees), while the other two are *obtuse* (more than 90 degrees). *Before the glue dries,* adjust the positions of the clamps or brace the corners to hold them square. If you're gluing up a large box, shift one or two of the clamps *slightly* so they are no longer parallel to the ends or sides, angling them toward the *acute* corners. *(SEE FIGURE 5-3.)* This will alter the direction of the force generated by the clamps and pull the corners back into alignment.

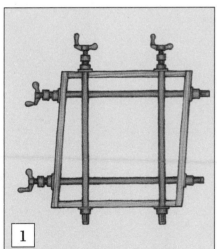

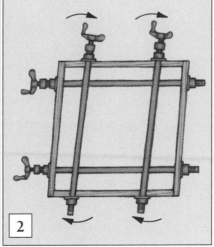

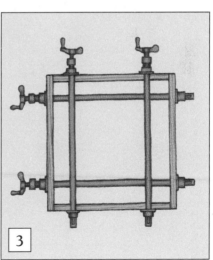

5-3 You can square up a large assembly by shifting the clamps. First, check the assembly with a square and find the two acute corners (1). Loosen one or two of the clamps and angle them slightly toward the acute corners (2). Slowly tighten the clamps, checking the corners often as you do so. When the clamps have pulled the assembly square, stop tightening (3).

Note: This technique will not work if the joinery is not square to begin with.

However, this trick only works for large boxes. If you're gluing up a small or medium-size box, clamp the assembly *diagonally,* from one acute corner to the other. *(See Figure 5-4.)* Or attach miter clamps to the corners to hold them square, provided these clamps don't interfere with the others. *(See Figure 5-5.)* You can also make *corner squares* — simple braces with one perfectly square corner — and attach them to the parts of the box that are out of alignment. *(See Figure 5-6.)*

To make sure that the box is flat, clamp it to a flat surface while the glue dries. You might use the top of your workbench (provided it's flat) or the work surface of your table saw (provided you unplug it and lower the blade). Or, you can use a *clamping grid* — a perfectly flat grid work made just for this purpose. *(See Figure 5-7.)* Old-time craftsmen sometimes used *winding sticks* to tell if an assembly was warped or twisted. They placed these long, straight sticks on top of the assembly and sighted across them. If the sticks looked parallel, the assembly was flat. *(See Figure 5-8.)*

TRY THIS TRICK

You can remove the warpage or twist from an assembly even after it's glued up, provided you've used a glue that will creep. (Both white and yellow PVA glues have this property.) Clamp or weight the assembly so it's twisted in the *opposite* direction and let it sit. The glue will allow the parts to creep back into alignment. Remove the clamps and check the assembly every few days. If it's still twisted, put it back in the clamps. Depending on the size of the assembly and the amount of warp, it can take anywhere from a few days to a few weeks to realign the parts.

5-4 To square up a small or medium-size box, straddle one or two bar clamps across the *acute* corners. Slowly tighten the clamps until the assembly is square. **Note:** Protect the corners with *corner cauls* — small blocks of wood with a V-shaped notch in one side. And remember, the joinery must be square in the first place for this to work.

5-5 You can also use miter clamps to hold the corners of small and medium-size boxes square. If the parts of the box are reasonably straight, you should only need two clamps. Fasten them across from one another diagonally, as shown.

5-6 If you don't have miter clamps, make several *corner squares*. These simple jigs have one perfectly square corner and two cleats so you can clamp them to an assembly. As with miter clamps, you only need to use two corner squares if you fasten them diagonally from one another on the assembly. (For plans on how to make corner squares, refer to "Clamping Aids" on page 69.)

5-7 To make sure that a box assembly is not warped or twisted, clamp it to a flat surface while the glue dries. Any level, rigid surface will do, but a clamping grid is specially designed for this purpose. The members of the grid are perfectly straight and flat, and the spaces between them make it easy for you to fasten down assemblies of all sizes. (For plans on how to build a clamping grid, refer to "Clamping Aids" on page 69.)

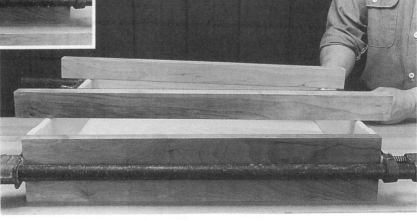

5-8 You can use *winding sticks* to tell if a drawer has a twist or "wind" in it. Lay two long, straight sticks across the top surfaces of the drawer and sight across them horizontally. If the sticks appear parallel to one another, the drawer is flat. If not, it's twisted.

ASSEMBLING FRAMES AND DOORS

Frame-and-panel joinery breaks a broad wooden surface into smaller parts so wood movement can be accommodated. The frame members — the *rails* and *stiles* — are glued to one another, while the panel (if there is one) floats in rabbets or grooves that have been cut into the rails and stiles.

The frame members can be assembled with many different types of joints — corner lap joints, miter joints, mortise-and-tenon joints, and dowel joints, just to name a few. But here again, the joinery isn't as important as the geometry. Most frames are rectangular constructions with square corners. The front and back surfaces of the frame members are parallel to and flush with one another. Consequently, when clamping the assembly together, you must hold the frame square and flat.

Bar clamps are useful for gluing up *most* large and medium-size frame-and-panel assemblies, provided the frame members aren't too slender and aren't mitered at the ends. If they're too slender, bar clamps may exert too much pressure, causing the rails and stiles to bow. If the frame is mitered, the bar clamps won't keep the miter joints from shifting. To assemble delicate frames or frames with mitered corners, use band clamps, miter clamps, or frame clamps. (*SEE FIGURES 5-9 AND 5-10.*)

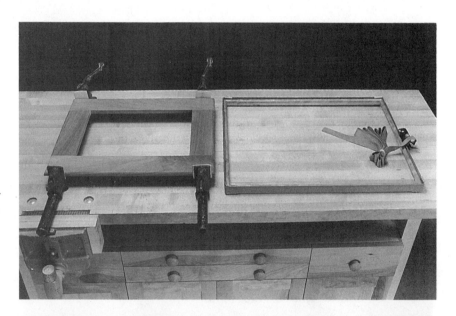

5-9 Bar clamps are handy when assembling sturdy frames, but they may generate too much pressure for frames with slender members. Excessive pressure may cause the rails and stiles to bow, and this may twist the assembly or pull the corners out of square. When gluing up delicate frames, choose light-duty clamps (such as band clamps) that will not distort the assembly.

5-10 One of the most adaptable and easy-to-use clamps for assembling mitered frames is a shop-made frame clamp. This holding jig keeps the members aligned and prevents the miter joints from slipping. It generates a moderate amount of pressure and distributes it to all four frame corners equally. You can increase or decrease the pressure on all four corners by turning a single handle. (For complete instructions on how to build this jig, refer to "Shop-Made Clamps," on page 88.)

To make sure the frames are square and flat when you clamp them up, you can employ techniques and equipment used for box assembly — particularly the clamping grid. Use this jig to square the frames *and* hold them flat. *(SEE FIGURE 5-11.)* A clamping grid is also helpful when assembling frames that aren't rectangular. *(SEE FIGURE 5-12.)*

5-11   In addition to using a clamping grid to hold a frame flat, you can also use it to square up a frame. Clamp a single rail or stile to the grid, grasp the opposite member, and shift the frame left or right until it's square (1). Then clamp all the frame members to the grid (2). Remember, the joinery must be square for this to work.

5-12   A clamping grid comes in handy when assembling odd-shaped frames and other unusual assemblies. Instead of trying to clamp the odd frame together, clamp the parts to the grid and let the grid hold it together.

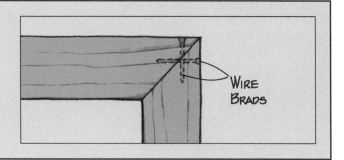

Try This Trick

Reinforce miter joints with wire brads or finishing nails. Use at least two nails per joint, and drive them from different directions so they cross one another, as shown. This will make it impossible to pull the joint apart, even if the glue doesn't hold.

WIRE BRADS

ASSEMBLING TABLES AND CHAIRS

In leg-and-rail constructions, the legs of a table or chair are joined to one another to hold them roughly vertical to the ground and to keep them from spreading. The legs of a table are usually joined by *aprons,* and the tabletop is joined to these aprons with cleats, screws (in pockets), or other devices. Usually, the cleats are slotted or the screw pockets are enlarged so the top can expand and contract. Chair legs are often

joined at several points by *stretchers* and *rungs,* while the seats are attached to the legs in many different ways, depending on the style of the chair.

Most tables and chairs are made up of at least eight major parts (four legs and four rails) and often incorporate many more. These parts are usually assembled with one or more types of mortise-and-tenon joints, and there can be more joints than there are parts. Fortunately, these joints don't have to be glued together all at once. Instead, most craftsmen find it easier to glue up two separate and roughly symmetrical halves, then join the halves. (*SEE FIGURES 5-13 AND 5-14.*) Use bar clamps or band clamps — whichever works best — for both steps.

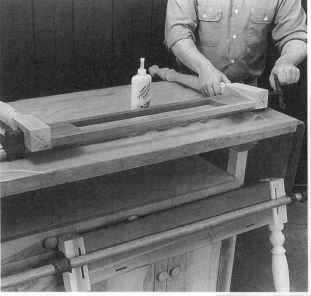

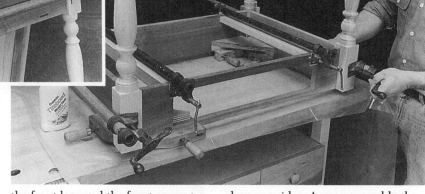

5-13 When gluing up a table, divide the assembly into two halves. How you divide the table depends on its design. Simple tables can be divided either front and back or left and right, but if the table incorporates a drawer (as does the table shown), it will be easier to assemble if you divide it into front and back halves. Glue up the back legs and back apron to make one half, and the front legs and the front apron to make the other. Let the glue dry on both subassemblies, then join the halves with the side aprons and drawer guides. As you assemble the two halves, be sure to keep the aprons square to one another. Also check that the drawer guides are parallel.

When the table or chair is assembled, all four legs must rest solidly on the floor. If the assembly is twisted even slightly, it will rock on two legs. You can correct this by removing a little stock from the end of one of the legs on which it rocks, but it's easier to avoid the problem altogether. As you assemble the halves, rest the legs on a flat surface until the glue dries. Once again, one of the handiest surfaces in your shop for this operation is your table saw. (*SEE FIGURE 5-15.*) Or fasten a scrap of plywood to a clamping grid to provide a broad, flat surface.

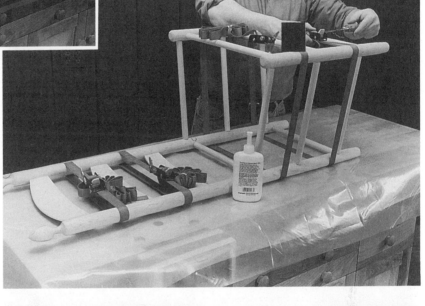

5-14 Unlike other common woodworking projects, chairs are not square or rectangular — many of the parts are joined at odd angles. Because of these angles, you must divide the chairs into left and right halves when assembling them. (If you divide them front and back, the angles of the side rungs will make it difficult — if not impossible — to join the halves.) Join each set of front and back legs with the side rungs, let the glue dry, then join the assembled halves with the remaining rungs and the chair back.

5-15 To make sure that tables and chairs aren't warped or twisted after you assemble the parts, rest them on a flat surface (such as the top of a table saw) while the glue dries. To use a table saw safely, unplug the machine, lower the blade beneath the surface, and cover the surface with a sheet of plastic to protect it from glue. In some cases, you may also have to remove the saw guard. Place the table or chair on the saw and check that all four legs rest solidly on the work surface. If the chair rocks slightly, weight down the legs that don't touch the surface until the glue has cured. If the chair rocks a lot, shift the clamps to help realign the parts.

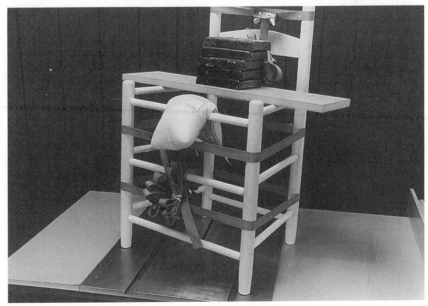

ASSEMBLING CABINETS AND BOOKCASES

A wooden case, such as a bookcase or a kitchen cabinet, often looks like a large box. But unlike a box, it supports shelves, doors, and drawers. Because of this, cases are among the most complex assemblies in woodworking.

Even so, case joinery is surprisingly simple. Many cases are joined with nothing more complicated than dadoes, grooves, and rabbets — there are just lots of them. The trick to assembling a case is to break it up into several smaller assemblies. Build each of them, then join the subassemblies. For example, a case often incorporates several frame-and-panel assemblies — the drawers may rest on web frames, and the doors are sometimes hung on face frames. Even the sides of

the case may be frames with panels. Assemble these frames first using the techniques described in "Assembling Frames and Doors" on page 62. Then glue together the frames and the other case parts. (SEE FIGURES 5-16 THROUGH 5-19.)

As when assembling other projects, you'll find that bar clamps and band clamps are the most useful tools for assembling cases. However, some cases don't need to be clamped at all. Instead, you can *nail* or *screw* the case together as you glue it up. These fasteners provide clamping pressure while the glue dries. Later, you can either remove the fasteners or leave them in place to reinforce the glue joints.

5-16 Because wooden cases are so complex, the glue-up procedure usually requires several steps. A typical kitchen cabinet, for example, must be glued up in four steps. First, assemble any subassemblies, such as a drawer support or a face frame. Make sure these are perfectly square; out-of-square parts will create problems in later steps.

5-17 Join a horizontal part to a case side to create a T-shaped assembly. Rest this assembly on its front edges — it will be stable enough to stand on its own. Add the remaining horizontal parts one by one, then join the second side.

5-18 Before the glue dries, check that the shelves and other horizontal parts are square to the sides. If they aren't, adjust the positions of the clamps, angling them toward the acute corners. Or attach a clamp diagonally from one acute corner to the other and slowly tighten it. When the clamp pulls the case square, attach the back to the case — this will hold the sides and shelves at 90 degrees to one another as the glue dries.

5-19 Turn the case assembly over on its back and attach the face frame. Make sure the face frame stiles are flush with the sides of the case and the top edges of the rails are flush with the shelves and drawer supports.

CONCEALING NAILS AND SCREWS

Craftsmen often use nails and screws as permanent miniature clamps. These fasteners align the adjoining parts, apply pressure while the glue cures, and reinforce the joint after the glue is cured. Unfortunately, fasteners sometimes detract from the appearance of a completed project. However, there are several ways to conceal them.

1 **The most effective way of** concealing fasteners is to drive them from *underneath* a shelf or tabletop or from *inside* a case. You won't see the fasteners when the project is complete. For example, if you need to fasten a shelf in a dado, drive the screw at an angle from underneath the shelf and into the side, as shown.

(continued) ▷

CONCEALING NAILS AND SCREWS — CONTINUED

2 **If you must drive a screw**
where it will be visible on the completed project, counterbore the screw hole so the head rests beneath the surface, then cover the head with a wooden plug. Cut this plug from scrap wood left over from the project, matching the wood species and color to the surrounding surface. As you glue the plug in the counterbore, carefully align the grain with the surrounding wood. When the plug is sanded flush, it should be nearly invisible.

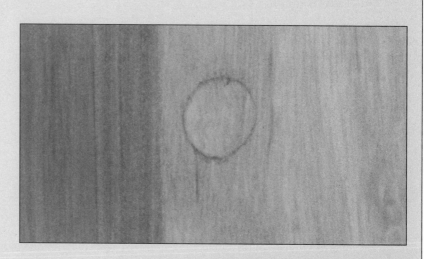

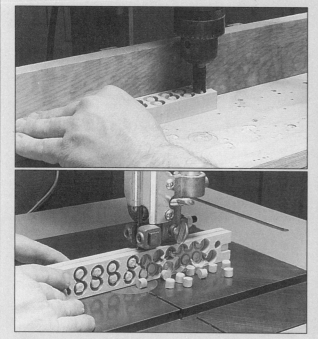

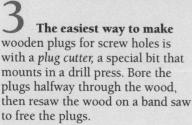

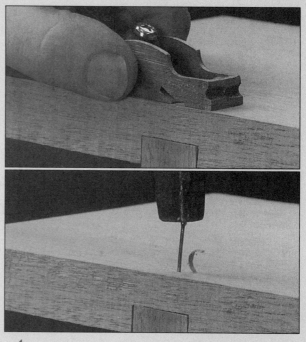

3 **The easiest way to make**
wooden plugs for screw holes is with a *plug cutter,* a special bit that mounts in a drill press. Bore the plugs halfway through the wood, then resaw the wood on a band saw to free the plugs.

4 **If you must drive a nail**
where it will be visible, use a *blind nail plane* to peel away a tiny sliver of wood from the surface. Drive the nail into the depression left by the sliver, set the head of the nail below the wood surface, and glue the sliver in place over the head of the nail. When you sand the surface clean, the nail will be invisible.

CLAMPING AIDS

No matter how large or diverse your selection of clamps, there are some gluing operations for which clamps alone aren't sufficient. Here are four additional fixtures to help hold the assembly as you glue it together.

1 A *pipe clamp rack* holds pipe clamps and prevents them from rolling over as you place boards in the clamps. The base of the rack also provides an easy-to-clean surface for gluing up small and medium-size projects — especially those that produce a lot of messy glue squeeze-out. The base is a laminated sink cutout (which you can purchase for just a few dollars at most building-supply stores and cabinet shops). Glue will not stick to this laminate; after each gluing operation, let the squeeze-out dry and peel it up.

2 A *clamping grid* provides a perfectly flat surface on which to assemble doors, drawers, and other assemblies which must remain flat as the glue dries. You can also use this fixture to help assemble odd-shaped projects. This particular grid is made from medium density fiberboard (called *MDF*) so it will remain perfectly stable. The feet on the grid are movable. If you find that one or more of the feet are in your way when clamping down a project, simply move them to other locations.

(continued) ▷

CLAMPING AIDS — CONTINUED

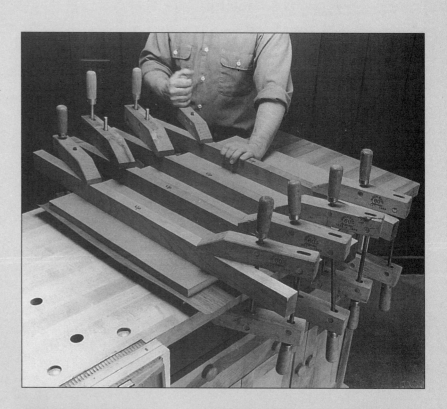

3 **A *press bar* is a thick wooden** beam, 2 or 3 feet long. It is *slightly* convex on one surface so you can apply pressure to the middle of a wide board. Place the press bar so that it stretches across the board with the convex surface against the wood. Clamp the bar down at the ends, as shown. As you tighten the clamps, the bar will flex slightly, distributing the pressure out from the middle and all along its length.

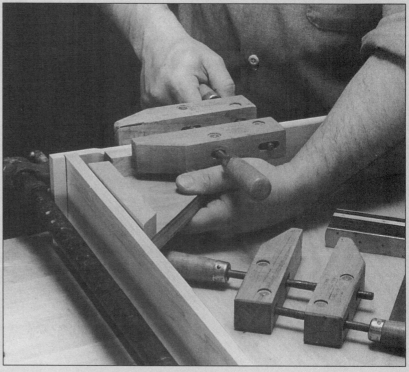

4 **A *corner square* is a** triangular jig with one perfectly square corner and cleats attached to the sides. These cleats allow you to fasten the jig to two boards that are joined at right angles. This, in turn, holds them perpendicular to one another.

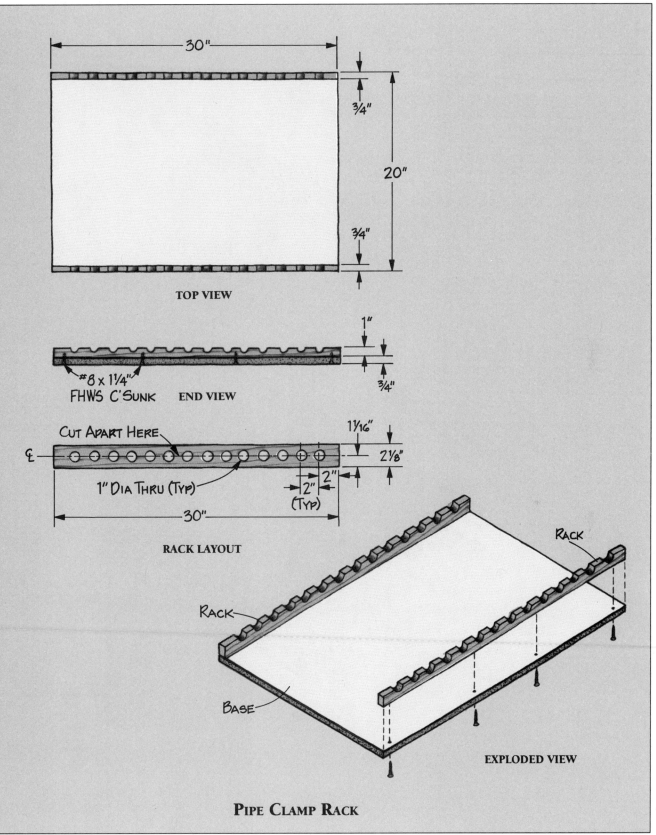

30"

3/4"

20"

3/4"

TOP VIEW

1"

3/4"

#8 x 1¼"
FHWS C'SUNK   **END VIEW**

CUT APART HERE

℄

1¼₆"

2⅛"

1" DIA THRU (TYP)

2"

2"
(TYP)

30"

RACK LAYOUT

RACK

RACK

BASE

EXPLODED VIEW

PIPE CLAMP RACK

(continued) ▷

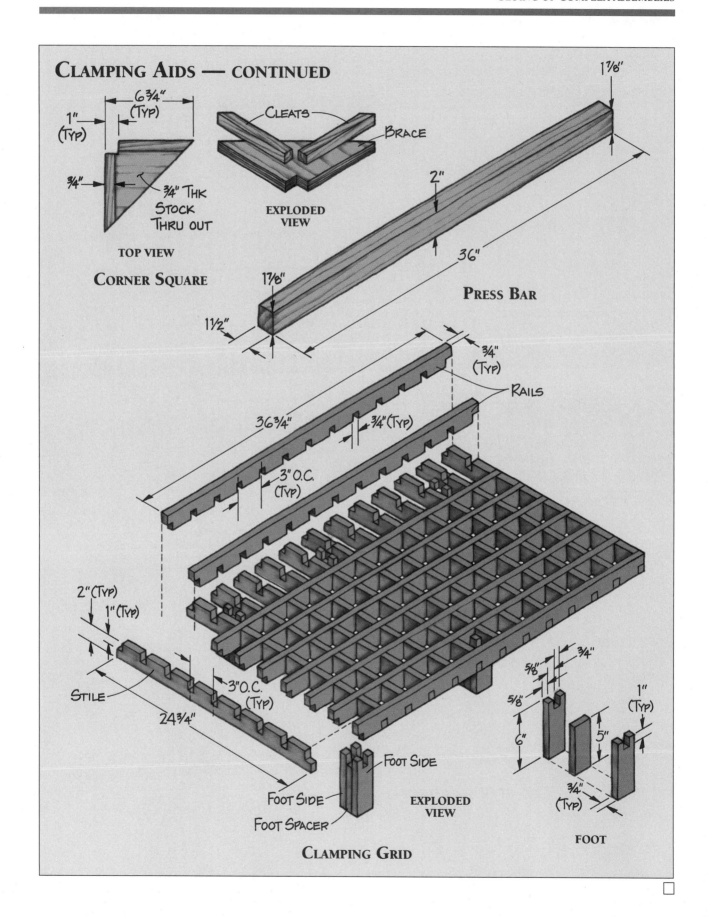

CLAMPING AIDS — CONTINUED

6¾" (TYP)

1" (TYP)

¾"

¾" THK STOCK THRU OUT

TOP VIEW

CORNER SQUARE

CLEATS

BRACE

EXPLODED VIEW

1⅞"

2"

36"

1⅞"

1½"

PRESS BAR

¾" (TYP)

RAILS

36¾"

¾" (TYP)

3" O.C. (TYP)

2" (TYP)

1" (TYP)

STILE

3" O.C. (TYP)

24¾"

FOOT SIDE

FOOT SIDE

FOOT SPACER

EXPLODED VIEW

5/8"

¾"

5/8"

6"

5"

1" (TYP)

¾" (TYP)

FOOT

CLAMPING GRID

6

VENEERING AND LAMINATING

Veneering is the art of disguising one wood species with another. When you veneer a piece, you glue thin slices of appealing (and oftentimes expensive) wood to a less-appealing (and less-expensive) surface. It's an old technique, almost as old as woodworking itself. Egyptian woodworkers first practiced veneering over 3,000 years ago!

Throughout its long history, craftsmen have developed different processes for applying veneer. Early veneers, which were very thick, were glued to the core material in the same manner as two boards glued face-to-face. Later, as new cutting tools enabled craftsmen to cut thinner and thinner veneer sheets, they developed special glues and gluing techniques to apply them.

The twentieth century saw another important development in the art — *plastic laminates*. These are thin sheets of paper, impregnated with plastic then heated and compressed to make them hard and durable. When glued to a surface, plastic laminates not only change the appearance of the project, but protect it against water, chemicals, and wear. The variety of plastic laminates, combined with many species of veneer and several types of adhesives give you an astounding selection of materials and methods for turning ordinary-looking surfaces into something extraordinary.

APPLYING VENEER

When you apply veneer to a wooden surface, you're actually gluing two pieces of wood face-to-face, even though one piece is much thinner than the other. You can use almost any glue for this operation, provided you have a way to clamp the thin veneer to the thicker substrate. This is what a veneer press does — it applies clamping pressure over a broad surface.

However, most small shops (and many large ones) can't afford the luxury of a veneer press and craftsmen have developed other gluing techniques to apply veneer. The most popular method is to use *contact cement.* This adhesive bonds on contact and needs no protracted clamping. All that's required is a brief application of pressure with a roller or a wooden block.

Contact cement is used to apply both regular veneer and paper-backed veneer. Regular veneer consists of extremely thin slices of solid wood, just $1/28$ inch thick. Paper-backed veneer is thinner still — just $1/64$ inch —

and must be glued to a paper backing to help it hold together. *(SEE FIGURE 6-1.)* Most woodworkers find that paper-backed veneer is easier to apply than regular veneer, but the thicker material is easier to sand and finish and is much more durable.

PREPARING AND CUTTING VENEER

When you purchase regular veneer, you'll likely find that the sheets are buckled. This is normal; the thin slices are not very stable until glued in place. Before you can apply the veneer to a substrate, you must flatten it. Wet it with a damp rag and press it between two $3/4$-inch plywood panels until you're ready to use it. The veneer should remain between the panels for at least three or four days to allow it to dry completely. *(SEE FIGURE 6-2.)*

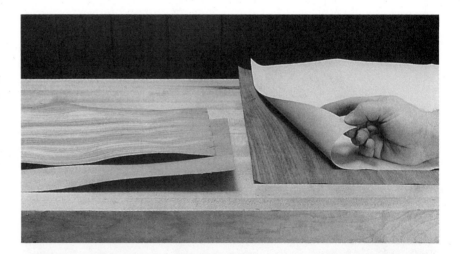

6-1 Most veneers are slices of solid wood $1/28$ inch thick. This is barely thick enough to hold together and too thin for the wood to be stable. Consequently, sheets of regular (unbacked) veneer tend to buckle and must be flattened before they can be used. Paper-backed veneer is sliced even thinner — just $1/64$ inch — and is glued to a sheet of stiff paper to hold the wood together and to keep it flat. Because it's so thin, paper-backed veneer is more flexible than regular veneer.

6-2 To flatten veneer, wet the sheets on both sides with a damp rag, then press them between two sheets of $3/4$-inch plywood for several days until they are completely dry. Place wrapping paper between the veneer sheets to help absorb the moisture. **Note:** Don't use newspaper; the ink may stain the veneer.

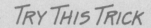

Try This Trick

If you aren't able to press the veneer for three or four days, you can use a steam iron to flatten it. Wipe *both* sides of the veneer with a damp rag, then press both sides with a dry (*no steam*) iron.

Inspect the surface you want to cover (called the *core material*) for dents, gouges, and other imperfections. Fill these defects with wood putty and sand them flush. (*See Figure 6-3.*) Measure the core material

and use either a veneer saw or a sharp knife to cut a piece of veneer slightly wider and longer than needed to cover it. (*See Figures 6-4 and 6-5.*) If you're using paper-backed veneer, cut it with a pair of scissors.

Try This Trick

When cutting a strip of veneer to cover an edge, make it about ⅛ inch wider than the board is thick. Wet the veneer on both sides to see which way it naturally wants to curl, and mark the concave side. Apply the strip with the *concave* side against the edge. If you glue it the other way around, the edges will want to pull away from the core.

6-3 The surface to which you apply the veneer must be perfectly smooth — any dents, gouges, or other defects will create depressions in the finished project. Fill any voids with stick shellac, wood putty, or even auto body putty (shown). Remember, because the surface will be hidden by veneer, it doesn't have to look good; it just has to be smooth.

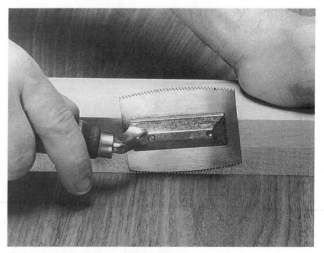

6-4 To cut veneer with a veneer saw, first lay a straightedge along the line you want to cut. Push or pull the saw across the veneer, using the straightedge as a guide. As you saw, press down very lightly. If you put too much pressure on the saw, it may dig in and tear the veneer. After several passes, the saw will cut through the veneer.

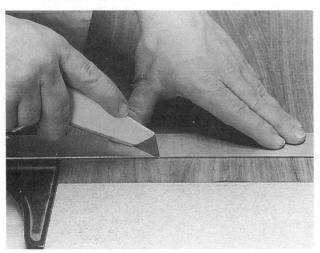

6-5 You can also use a sharp knife to cut veneer, guiding it with a straightedge. However, this method works best when cutting *across* the wood grain. When you cut with the grain, the knife may act as a wedge and split the thin wood. It also tends to follow the grain unless you keep it pressed firmly against the straightedge.

MATCHING AND JOINING VENEER

On occasion, you may have to join two or more pieces of veneer to make a sheet large enough to cover a surface, to create a decorative effect, or both. To do this, first *match* the pieces — that is, orient the sheets the way you want to join them.

To match veneers, you should purchase sheets that all come from the same log or *flitch*. Ideally, they should be arranged or numbered in the order in which they were cut. Otherwise, all you can do is make a *random match* — that is, arrange the sheets side by side so the wood grain and color look continuous, just as if you were gluing boards of random widths edge to edge.

If the sheets of veneer are all from the same flitch, there are many different patterns you can create. You might simply arrange them side by side in the order in which they were cut, creating a *slip match*. Or open the flitch like the pages of a book, creating a *book match*. Or you can cut four sheets at an angle, then arrange them so the angled wood grain forms a *diamond match*. FIGURE 6-6 shows several ways to match veneers.

Once you have decided how to match the veneer, you must *joint* it, just as you joint boards before you glue them edge to edge. The easiest way to joint veneer is

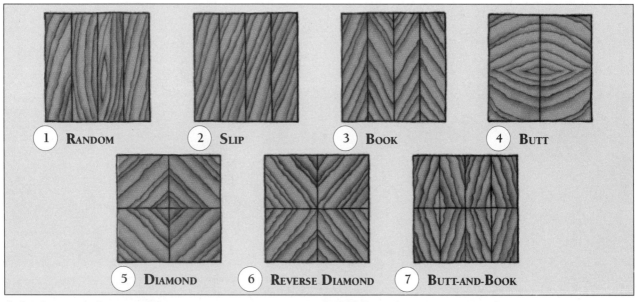

6-6 If you purchase random sheets of veneer and need to join them, make a *random match* (1) — that is, simply arrange them for the best effect. If the sheets were all sliced from the same log and you know the approximate order in which they were cut, you can create geometric patterns with the wood grain, such as the *slip match* (2), *book match* (3), *butt match* (4), *diamond match* (5), and *reverse diamond match* (6). You can even combine patterns, such as the *butt-and-book match* (7).

to overlap the sheets where you want to butt them together, then cut through both sheets at once. *(See Figure 6-7.)* After jointing, temporarily assemble the

sheets by splicing them with masking tape or gummed veneer tape. *(See Figure 6-8.)* In some cases, you may want to tape *and* glue the seams. *(See Figure 6-9.)*

For Your Information

Veneer joints don't have to be straight; they can be curved or even intricately shaped. To cut a curved or shaped veneer joint, overlap two or more pieces of veneer, taping *all* the pieces to a sheet of posterboard so they won't shift as you cut. Cover the veneer pieces with a second sheet of posterboard to protect

them. Lay out the joint on the posterboard and cut it with a jigsaw or scroll saw. When you remove the posterboard and the tape, the edges will match perfectly. This, in fact, is an important technique in *marquetry,* the art of making pictures and designs with contrasting colors of veneer.

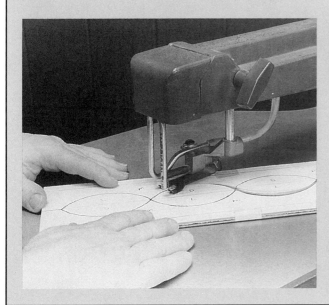

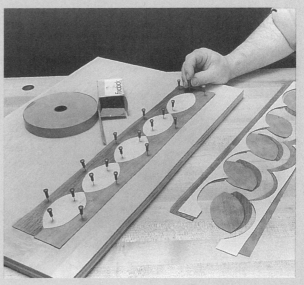

6-7 To joint two pieces of veneer, overlap the edges you want to join. Tape the pieces together on both the front and back faces so they won't slip, then cut through *both* sheets at the same time. Even if you don't make a perfectly straight cut, the edges should match perfectly.

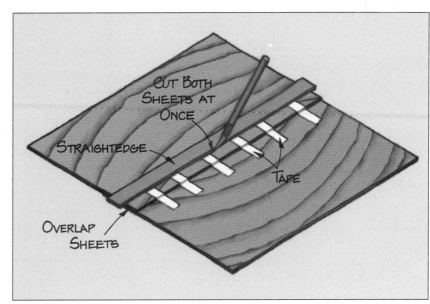

6-8 You must assemble the
sheets *before* gluing them to the core
material. Arrange them *good side up*
on the surface you want covered (or
on a sheet of plywood), holding them
in place with veneer pins. (These
look like push pins but are sharper
and leave smaller holes.) Make sure
the edges butt together with no gaps,
then cover the seams with masking
tape or gummed veneer tape. When
you remove the pins, the sheets
should be joined. **Note:** Many craftsmen prefer gummed tape to masking
tape because it's easy to remove and
gentle on the veneer — simply wet
it with a damp rag and peel it off.
There's little danger that you might
pull up a sliver of veneer with this
tape.

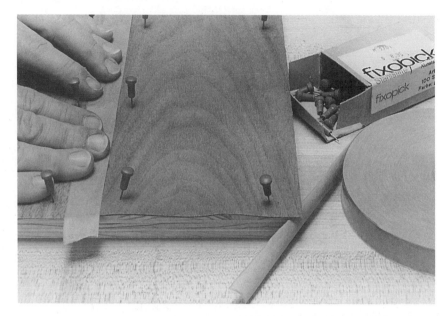

6-9 If you wish, you can glue
the sheets together to make stronger
seams. Fold the pieces of veneer
where they are taped together to
expose the jointed edges. Carefully
apply glue to one edge, then open
the sheets so the assembly is flat
again. Wipe off any excess glue that
squeezes out of the seam with a rag.
Don't worry about glue stains — this
is the side of the veneer that will
face *down*.

APPLYING AND TRIMMING VENEER

To apply the veneer, first make sure the area in which
you're working is *clean* — any dust will weaken the
glue bond. If you wish to apply veneer to more than
one surface of a project, plan to cover the vertical surfaces first, then the horizontal areas. For instance, if
you're veneering a tabletop, cover the ends and edges,
then the face. This arrangement looks and wears better than the other way around.

When covering solid wood, plan to apply the veneer
so the wood grain of both the veneer and the core are
parallel. For plywood, attach the veneer with the wood

grain *perpendicular* to the top ply. If you're covering
particleboard, the grain direction of the veneer
doesn't matter.

Once you've decided in what order you will cover
the surfaces and how to orient the veneer, apply contact cement to both the veneer *and* the core material.
(*SEE FIGURE 6-10.*) Use a brush to cover small areas and
a paint roller for large ones. Let the glue dry until it
loses its shine and looks dull. (For most brands of
contact cement, this takes 10 to 15 minutes.) Test it
with your finger — it should no longer feel tacky.

A SAFETY REMINDER

Use *water-based* contact cement; fumes from the solvent-based variety are toxic and extremely flammable. If you must use solvent-based contact cement, don't work around open flames (including the pilot lights in gas stoves, furnaces, and water heaters). Keep the shop doors and windows open for extra ventilation.

Position the veneer directly over the core material, but keep the glue-covered surfaces from touching. Lay dowels, wood strips, or paper strips across the core and rest the veneer on these spacers. *(SEE FIGURE 6-11.)* Working from one edge (or from the middle out toward the sides), remove the spacers one at a time and press the veneer against the core material. To eliminate air bubbles and to ensure that the bond is complete, apply pressure to the entire surface with a veneer roller or a rolling pin. *(SEE FIGURE 6-12.)* Finally, trim the overhanging veneer with a veneer saw or a sharp knife. *(SEE FIGURE 6-13.)*

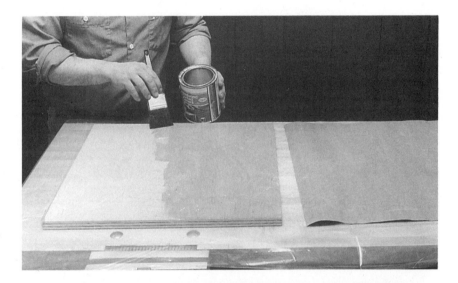

6-10 **Apply a thin, even layer of** contact cement to *both* surfaces that you want to bond — the veneer and the core material. Be careful to cover the surfaces evenly and completely in *one* pass with the brush or roller — don't try to spread out the glue or go over an area a second time. The partially dried glue will start to ball up, and you'll find it impossible to get rid of the lumps. Let the glue dry on both surfaces until it's no longer tacky.

6-11 **Because the contact cement** bonds on contact, it's important that you position the veneer *precisely* before you press it down on the core material. To do this, lay dowel rods, wood strips, or paper strips across the core every 6 to 12 inches to serve as spacers. Rest the veneer on the spacers and position it above the core. Remove a single spacer, then *lightly* press a small amount of the veneer against the core. Check that the veneer is where you want it to be — if not, you can dissolve the glue bond with acetone (or whatever solvent the glue manufacturer recommends) and try again. When you're certain the veneer is positioned correctly, remove the spacers one at a time. Work from one edge to the other or from the middle out toward the sides, pressing down the veneer as you go.

6-12 You can't generate enough pressure with your hands to create a strong glue bond between the veneer and the core. You may also leave a few air bubbles under the veneer, and some areas may not bond at all. So after you've pressed the veneer in place, roll it out with a veneer roller or a rolling pin. Put as much pressure as you possibly can on the roller, and make sure you roll the entire surface.

6-13 When the veneer is bonded to the core, turn the assembly over on a sheet of plywood. Using the edge of the core material as a guide, trim the overhanging veneer with a sharp knife or a veneer saw. Cut *across* the end grain first, then cut *with* the grain along the edges. This will keep the veneer from splitting at the corners. **Note:** You can also use a router and a flush-trim bit to trim the veneer — *if you're careful!* A router may chip or tear out the delicate veneer, so make sure the bit is sharp and feed the router very slowly. Once again, trim the ends first, then the edges.

ALTERNATIVE VENEERING METHODS

Although contact cement is the most popular material for applying veneer, it isn't the only material. There are several other adhesives that do not require massive veneer presses or intricate clamping techniques.

Hot hide glue — Before the development of contact cement, individual craftsmen and small shops applied veneer with hot hide glue, a laundry iron, and a special *veneer hammer.* To apply veneer using the old hammer-veneering technique, cover both the veneer and the core material with fresh, hot hide glue. Let the glue cool slightly and position the veneer over the core. Wipe a small area of the veneer (about 2 or 3 square feet) with a damp rag and iron it to reheat the glue. Using the broad end of the veneer hammer, press the veneer down, rubbing *with* the grain. Keep rubbing until the glue cools. As the temperature drops, the glue will develop a great deal of tack, enough to hold

the veneer flat until the adhesive cures completely. (*SEE FIGURES 6-14 AND 6-15.*) Repeat this procedure until the entire sheet of veneer is bonded to the core.

Hot-melt adhesive — Manufacturers of hot-melt glue make this adhesive in large, thin sheets for veneering. Compared to other glues, hot-melt sheets are fairly expensive, but they eliminate a lot of the mess normally associated with veneering. They also allow you to put the veneer right where you want it.

The glue sheets come with a paper backing. Place a sheet on the core material with the paper up. Using a laundry iron, heat the sheet so it sticks to the core. Let it cool, then peel off the backing. Position the veneer over the core, then iron the veneer to melt the glue for a second time. As soon as the adhesive cools again, it will bond the veneer to the core. (*SEE FIGURE 6-16.*)

6-14 To apply veneer with hot
hide glue, cover both the veneer and
the core material with adhesive. Let
the glue cool and position the veneer
over the core. You can shift the
veneer to position it precisely even
after it touches the core. Unlike contact cement, hide glue does not bond
on contact. If necessary, hold the
veneer in place with veneer pins.
Wipe a small section of the veneer
with a damp rag, then heat it with
a laundry iron to soften the glue.
Note: The water helps to keep the
iron from burning the wood. However, be careful not to use too much,
since water may weaken the glue
bond.

6-15 When the glue is hot, rub
the veneer with the broad, flat edge
of a veneer hammer. Stroke the
wood *with* the grain; if you draw the
hammer across the grain, the wood
will stretch and split. Keep rubbing
until the glue is cool and you have
squeezed as much adhesive as you
can out from under the veneer. At
this point, the hide glue becomes
tacky enough to hold the veneer flat
on the core. Repeat for other areas
until the entire sheet is bonded. Let
the glue dry for at least 24 hours.

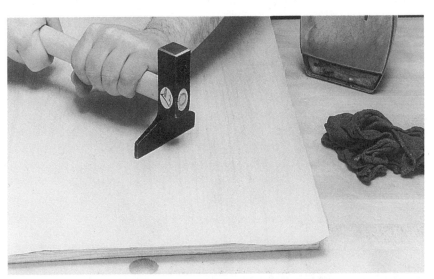

6-16 To apply veneer with sheets
of hot-melt adhesive, you must heat
the glue *twice* — once to bond the
glue sheet to the core (as shown),
then a second time to bond the
veneer to the adhesive. Use an ordinary laundry iron as a heat source
for both steps. Wipe the veneer with
a damp rag before heating it and be
careful not to get the iron so hot that
it burns the veneer.

Peel-and-stick veneer — Perhaps the easiest kind of veneer to apply is peel-and-stick — strips or sheets of paper-backed veneer with a pressure-sensitive adhesive on the back. The strips are handy for covering the exposed edges of plywood; the sheets may be used to cover broader surfaces. Just peel the paper off the back to expose the adhesive, then stick the veneer to the wood. Roll the veneer with a veneer roller or a rolling pin — the pressure is necessary to form a strong glue bond. (SEE FIGURE 6-17.)

APPLYING PLASTIC LAMINATES

The term *plastic laminate* is something of a misnomer; this material is actually multiple layers of resin-soaked paper hot-pressed together. The top layer of paper is colored or printed with a decorative design, while the phenolic resin that binds the papers together is waterproof and highly resistant to chemicals, heat, and wear. These features have made plastic laminate a popular protective coating for all sorts of furniture and built-ins, especially kitchen and bathroom cabinets.

There are five types of plastic laminate commonly available:

■ *General-purpose* laminate is $1/16$ inch thick and used for surfaces that see a good deal of wear and tear, such as the tops and edges of counters.

■ *Vertical-surface* laminate is $1/32$ inch thick and used for the sides and other outside surfaces of cabinets that see less wear.

■ *Post-forming* laminate will conform to curved surfaces if warmed with a heat gun as you fit it to a project.

■ *Backing* laminate is just .020 inch thick and does not come in colors or designs. It's sometimes applied to the back of a panel to keep it from warping. (SEE FIGURE 6-18.)

■ *Liner* laminate is similar to backing laminate, but it's available in either white or colors. It's often used to line the interiors of cabinets.

These products are usually applied to manufactured wood products — particleboard, medium density fiberboard, and hardwood plywood — rather than to solid wood. Wood and softwood plywood are rarely used because they're too unstable — they expand and contract too much. Softwood plywood often has gaps and voids in the surface, and these will create depressions in the laminate. Furthermore, some softwood plywoods (such as Douglas fir) have strong grain patterns with high and low spots. These *telegraph* through the laminate and become visible under the right lighting conditions.

No matter what type of laminate or core material you use, the two are usually bonded together with contact cement. The technique for applying laminate is very much like veneering, with a few important exceptions.

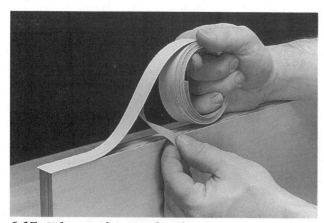

6-17 When applying peel-and-stick veneer, peel off the paper as you go — don't peel away all the paper from the piece before sticking it to the core. By peeling away the paper a little at a time, you reduce the chance that the adhesive will become contaminated with dust. This helps to ensure a strong bond.

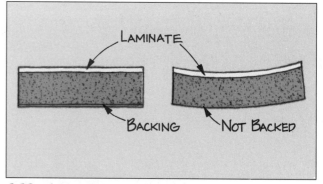

6-18 If you apply a laminate to an *unsupported* panel — one without a frame or brace work — chances are that it will warp. The unprotected side absorbs and releases moisture faster than the side with the laminate, making it expand and contract more. To prevent warping, apply a backing laminate or liner to the other side of the panel so both sides will move at the same rate.

CUTTING LAMINATES

Laminate comes in 4-foot-wide, 8-foot-long sheets and must be cut to size. Usually, you want to cut the laminate slightly larger than the area you're covering, but if you're covering the inside of a cabinet, you may have to fit it precisely. There are several tools you can use to cut laminate:

■ A table saw with a *plywood blade* works well. A carbide-tipped blade with a triple-chip grind performs best and stays sharp longer, but a high-speed steel blade will do. Use a zero-clearance insert to prevent chipping.

■ Probably the most versatile tool for cutting laminate is a *router with a carbide-tipped straight bit.* Not only can you cut the laminate with a router, you can joint edges as well. (*See Figures 6-19 and 6-20.*)

■ Many professional cabinetmakers use a *scoring cutter* to scratch a line in the laminate, then snap it along the line. (*See Figure 6-21.*)

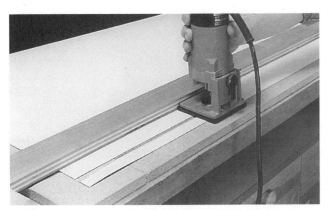

6-19 To cut laminate with a router and a straight bit, first place a sheet of plywood over your workbench to protect it. Lay the laminate on the plywood, and position a straightedge over the laminate. Clamp the straightedge and the laminate to the plywood, then rout through the laminate, using the straightedge as a guide. **Note:** Always rout the laminate with the face side *down.* This will protect it from scratches.

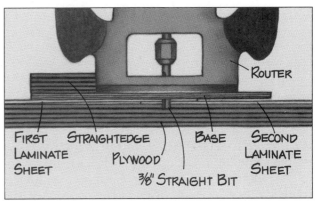

6-20 To join two sheets of laminate, you must joint the edges. Lap the sheets where you want to joint them; then rout them, cutting through *both* sheets at the same time. The routed edges will mate perfectly. Assemble the sheets *before* applying them, taping the seams together on the face side of the laminate.

6-21 A scoring cutter makes quick and easy work of cutting sheets of laminate to size. Using a straightedge to guide the cutter, press down hard and score a line in the colored or *face* side of the laminate. If necessary, repeat several times until you've cut a deep, continuous groove. Then bend the laminate, folding the face side (the side with the pattern or color) in on itself. The laminate will break cleanly along the scored groove.

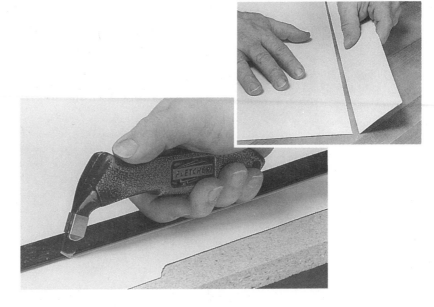

GLUING AND TRIMMING LAMINATES

When applying the laminate, you usually want to cover the vertical surface or the edges first, then the horizontal surfaces. The horizontal laminates will lap the edges of the vertical ones. This arrangement helps to prevent spilled water and chemicals from penetrating the seams.

Spread glue on the core material *and* the back of the laminate. Wait for the glue to dry, then position the laminate over the core and press it in place. To help position large sheets, use dowels, wood strips, or paper strips as spacers to keep the two materials separated until you're ready to press the laminate against the core. Once the laminate is pressed in place, apply pressure over the entire surface with a veneer roller or a rolling pin, then *pound* the surface with a mallet and a block of wood. (SEE FIGURE 6-22.)

Use a router and a trimming bit to cut the laminate to size after it's bonded to the core. When trimming parts with edges that will later be covered by another sheet of laminate (such as the strips that cover the banding around the circumference of a countertop), use a *flush-trim* bit. When trimming parts that lap over the edge of another piece of laminate (such as the tops of counters), use a *bevel-trim* bit. (SEE FIGURES 6-23 AND 6-24.) If you can't reach a portion of the laminate with the router, use a fine flat file to trim it to size.

6-22 Because laminate is so much harder and thicker than veneer (and hard, stiff materials distribute the pressure over a broader area), rolling the laminate may not produce enough pressure to create the strongest possible bond. To ensure that the laminate is properly bonded to the core, *pound* the surface to generate the necessary pressure. Place a block of wood over the laminate to protect it, then hit the block with a mallet. Move the block a few inches and repeat. Continue until you have pounded the entire surface.

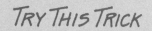

TRY THIS TRICK

To reattach laminate that has separated from the core material, use a laundry iron to melt the glue. Cover the laminate with a thin cloth or several sheets of newspaper to keep it from being scorched, then iron the surface. Clamp the laminate to the core until the glue cools.

FLUSH-TRIM BIT

SELF EDGE

6-23 When covering a countertop with plastic laminate, begin with the edges or *bandings*. Apply oversize strips of laminate to these vertical surfaces, then cut them to size with a router and *flush-trim* bit. The bit trims the laminate flush with the wood surface and cuts the edges at 90 degrees, as shown. This is necessary to create a tight joint between the vertical pieces (called *self edges*) and the horizontal piece that will cover the countertop.

6-24 After trimming the self
edges, cover the horizontal surface
of the countertop with an oversize
sheet of laminate. Trim this sheet to
size with a *bevel-trim* bit. This will
cut the laminate to size *and* bevel
the edge at either a 10- or 15-degree
angle. A beveled edge feels softer
and won't chip as easily. For an
even softer edge, *lightly* file the arris,
rounding over the edge of the horizontal laminate. **Note:** *Don't* attempt
to trim a piece of laminate that laps
the edge of another with a flush-trim

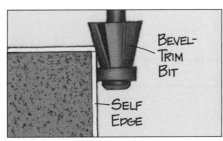

bit. If the router tips, even a little,
the cutter will dig into the lapped
laminate, scraping away the color or
the design.

Veneer- and Laminate-Cutting Jigs

If you do a lot of work with veneer or laminate,
you may want to build special jigs to help cut these
materials quickly and accurately.

1 Make the base of the veneer-
cutting jig from plywood or particleboard, and joint a clear piece of
hardwood for the straightedge. Mount
the straightedge to the base with carriage bolts, washers, wing nuts, and
springs, as shown. To use the veneer-
cutting jig, loosen the wing nuts and
allow the springs to raise the straightedge. Slide the veneer under the
straightedge, then lock it down with
the wing nuts. Cut the veneer with a
veneer saw or utility knife, using the
straightedge as a guide.

2 Make the straightedge for
the laminate-cutting jig by ripping
a 3-inch-wide strip from a sheet of
³/₄-inch cabinet-grade hardwood
plywood — the *factory edge* cut by
the manufacturer is usually very
straight. Glue this to a base — a
strip of ¹/₄-inch plywood 3 inches
wider than the sole of your router —
and rout a long groove in the base
with the same straight bit you will
use to cut the laminate. To position
the jig on the laminate, line up the
inside edge of the groove with the
line that you want to cut.

(continued) ▷

VENEER- AND LAMINATE-CUTTING JIGS — CONTINUED

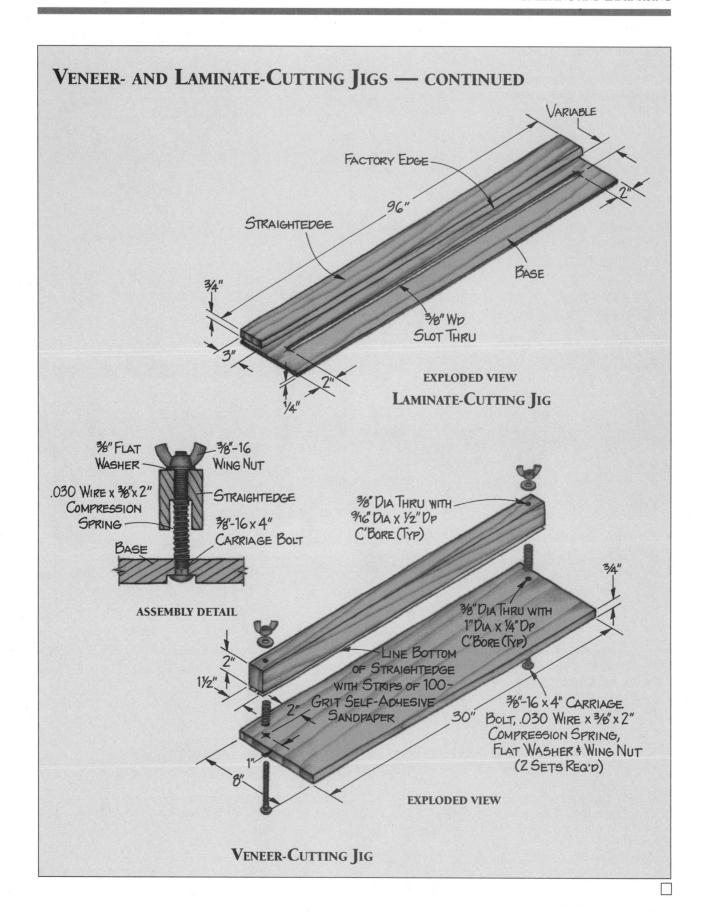

VARIABLE

FACTORY EDGE

96"

STRAIGHTEDGE

2"

BASE

3/4"

3/8" WD SLOT THRU

3"

2"

1/4"

EXPLODED VIEW

LAMINATE-CUTTING JIG

3/8" FLAT WASHER

3/8"-16 WING NUT

.030 WIRE x 3/8"x 2" COMPRESSION SPRING

STRAIGHTEDGE

3/8"-16 x 4" CARRIAGE BOLT

BASE

ASSEMBLY DETAIL

3/8" DIA THRU WITH 9/16" DIA x 1/2" DP C'BORE (TYP)

3/4"

3/8" DIA THRU WITH 1" DIA x 1/4" DP C'BORE (TYP)

2"

1 1/2"

2"

LINE BOTTOM OF STRAIGHTEDGE WITH STRIPS OF 100-GRIT SELF-ADHESIVE SANDPAPER

30"

3/8"-16 x 4" CARRIAGE BOLT, .030 WIRE x 3/8" x 2" COMPRESSION SPRING, FLAT WASHER & WING NUT (2 SETS REQ'D)

1"

8"

EXPLODED VIEW

VENEER-CUTTING JIG

PROJECTS

7

SHOP-MADE CLAMPS

A workshop corollary to Murphy's Law declares, "You always need one more clamp than you have." It's true — clamps are expensive enough that few craftsmen can afford to equip their shops all at once. Instead, most purchase one or two clamps at a time and always seem to be (at least) one short.

There is a solution to this problem — you can make your own clamps, often for less than a quarter of the expense of the store-bought variety! They are not difficult to make, since there is rarely more than one moving part. Nor is the construction time-consuming, particularly if you set up to make several clamps at once.

Are shop-made clamps less effective than those you can purchase? With the aid of Shopsmith, Inc., a tool manufacturer in Dayton,

Ohio, we tested all the clamps you see here and found that, on the average, they generated about two-thirds as much pressure as their store-bought relatives. Since you rarely use all the pressure that a clamp can exert, this shouldn't hamper your woodworking. If the projects you like to build require lots of clamping pressure, just make more clamps!

Clamping Mechanisms

We have used three common mechanisms to exert pressure in the shop-made clamps shown in this chapter:

- Wooden screws
- Threaded metal rods or bolts
- Cams

Wooden screws require a die to cut the male screw threads and a matching tap to cut the female threads. Tap-and-die sets are available in various diameters from most mail-order woodworking suppliers. Purchase a large size, ³/₄ inch or more in diameter — the larger the diameter of the screw, the more durable it is. All the clamps with wooden threads shown in this chapter have 1-inch-diameter screws.

Cutting wooden threads is straightforward, but it takes a knack. You must not feed the tap or the die too fast or you might tear out the wood. Furthermore, you must *lubricate* the tap and die with boiled linseed oil as you cut. (*See Figures 7-1 and 7-2.*) This, too, helps to prevent the wood from tearing.

Occasionally, you must *capture* the end of a screw in the movable jaw, making a rotary joint between the two pieces. For instance, the end of the wooden screw in the pipe clamp is captured in the jaw. As you turn the screw, the jaw moves back and forth — but the jaw doesn't turn with the screw. To make this special joint, you must cut a round groove in the end of the screw. (*See Figures 7-3 and 7-4.*) Drill two holes in the jaw. Make the first hole the same diameter as the end of the screw and the second the same diameter as the round groove. The second hole should intersect the first, as shown in *Figure 7-5*. Insert the end of the screw in the first hole, and drive a dowel through the second.

7-2 Cut the mating threads for the screw in a similar manner, using the tap. Drill a hole in the *nut* — the board that will hold the female threads. This hole must be slightly smaller than the diameter of the screw. (Check the instructions that come with the tap and die for the precise diameter.) Lubricate the sides of the hole with linseed oil. Press the tap into the hole, turning it as you do so. You'll find that the tap requires a good deal more effort to turn than the die, so choose a wrench with a lot of leverage, such as a breaker bar (shown). As you work, continue to lubricate the hole with linseed oil.

7-1 Use a die to cut the screw threads. Make sure that the diameter of the dowel is slightly smaller than the hole in the die. Saturate the dowel with linseed oil to lubricate it, then press the die onto the end of the rod, turning the die as you do so. Keep the dowel flooded with linseed oil as you cut the threads.

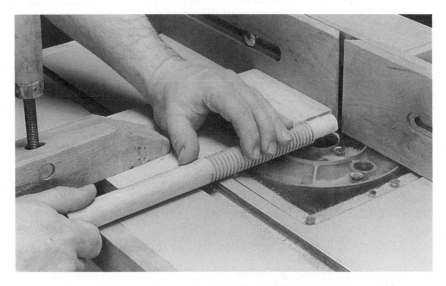

7-3 To cut a round groove near the end of a wooden screw, use a table-mounted router and a straight bit. First, cut a smooth area at the end of the screw. Raise the bit just a fraction of an inch above the table. Use the fence to control the length of the smooth area, and clamp a block of scrap wood to the table, perpendicular to the fence, to guide the screw. Turn on the router, then feed the screw over the bit, rotating it slowly as you cut. Stop when the end of the screw butts against the fence.

7-4 Readjust the depth of cut so the bit protrudes about an inch above the table. Again, use the fence as a stop, this time to determine how far the groove will be from the end of the screw, and position the scrap wood to control the depth of the groove. To cut the groove, turn the router on, place the end of the screw against the fence, and carefully roll the screw against the scrap wood block. Rotate the screw one full revolution, keeping its smooth end firmly against the fence and the threads against the block.

7-5 To capture the end of the screw in the jaw, drill a stopped hole in the jaw the same diameter as the smooth end of the screw. Drill a smaller hole through the jaw, the same diameter as the groove in the screw end, perpendicular to the stopped hole. This through hole should intersect the stopped hole, but the two holes must be offset slightly. Insert the screw in the stopped hole, then drive a dowel into the through hole. This will pin the jaw to the screw.

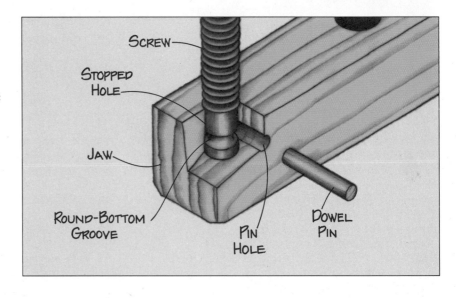

Threaded metal rods and bolts are available at most hardware stores. Threaded rod (also called *all-thread*) is commonly sold in diameters from ⅛ to ½ inch and lengths of 3 and 4 feet. Bolts are available in the same diameters, although the lengths are limited. The longest all-thread carriage bolts (bolts that are threaded from the head to the tip) are just 7 inches long, and the longest all-thread hex head bolts are 6 inches long.

You can use a variety of nuts with the threaded rod and bolts — hex nuts, square nuts, wing nuts, T-nuts,

even plastic knobs with nuts imbedded in them. *(See Figure 7-6.)* The type of nut you use depends on how you want to apply the pressure.

On some shop-made clamps, you must fashion a wooden handle to turn a bolt or a length of all-thread. This handle can be a circle, an oval, or a lever — any shape that fits your hand comfortably and affords you a good grasp. *(See Figure 7-7.)* There are also plastic handles available at many hardware stores and through mail-order suppliers.

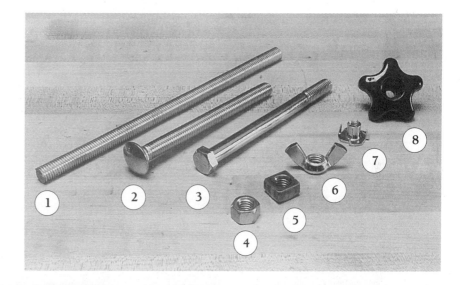

7-6 Hardware stores usually carry several types of nuts and bolts that you can use to generate clamping pressure: threaded rod, or *all-thread* (1), an *all-thread carriage bolt* (2), an *all-thread hex head bolt* (3), a *hex nut* (4), a *square nut* (5), a *wing nut* (6), a *T-nut* (7), and a *threaded knob* (8).

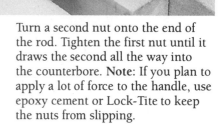

7-7 To fasten a wooden handle to the end of a threaded rod, drill a counterbore in the handle the same depth as the nut is thick and a little smaller in diameter than the nut is wide. Drill a hole the same diameter as the rod through the center of this

counterbore. Turn a nut onto one end of the rod and continue turning until the nut is 1 or 2 inches from the rod end. Place a flat washer over the nut, then insert the rod through the handle. The counterbore in the handle must face the end of the rod.

Turn a second nut onto the end of the rod. Tighten the first nut until it draws the second all the way into the counterbore. **Note:** If you plan to apply a lot of force to the handle, use epoxy cement or Lock-Tite to keep the nuts from slipping.

FOR YOUR INFORMATION

You can calculate the amount of pressure (P) that a bolt or threaded rod will exert, provided you know the distance between the individual threads (T), the radius (R) of the handle or lever, and the force (F) you can apply to it:

$$P = (F \times R \times 6.2832) \div T$$

You rarely need to use this formula when designing a clamp, but it does tell you something valu-able. The pressure you can apply depends not on the diameter of the threaded rod, but on the force with which you turn it, the size of the handle, and (to a lesser extent) the pitch of the threads. If you need more pressure but can't apply more force, make a bigger handle or use a threaded rod with a finer thread pitch.

Cams work on the same principle as wedges. In fact, a cam is nothing more than a wedge wound around a pivot. *(SEE FIGURE 7-8.)* As you look at a cam from the top, it's roughly circular in shape with a protruding lever that allows you to turn it easily. The pivot hole is slightly off-center, making one side of the cam closer to the pivot than the other. If you position the cam with the close side resting against a surface and then turn it so the opposite side comes in contact with that same surface, the cam will press against the surface with considerable force.

It's easy to make a cam from wood. Choose a dense, hard wood such as maple, oak, or hickory — these will wear better than softer woods. Lay out the cam with the pivot off-center. *(SEE FIGURE 7-9.)* Just how far off-center depends on how far you want the edge of the cam to move. The farther off-center the pivot is, the farther the edge travels.

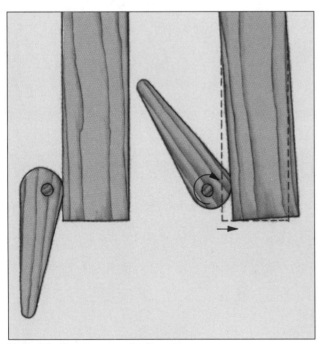

7-8 The business end of a cam is round, and the pivot is slightly off-center, making one side of the cam closer to the pivot than the other. When you rotate the cam, it wedges itself between the pivot and whatever surface it's resting against. This, in turn, applies pressure to that surface.

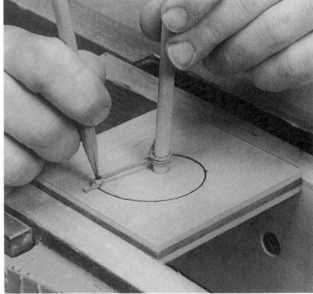

7-9 Here is an easy way to lay out a cam. Wind a string around a round object such as a dowel. Tie the free end of the string to a pencil. Mark the pivot and the closest point of the cam to the pivot on the stock. Place the dowel on the pivot mark and swing the pencil around it, unwinding the string as you go. The line you draw will get progressively farther away from the pivot as the string unwinds.

TRADITIONAL HAND SCREW

These shop-made hand screws have a long reach and a large capacity, and they generate a great deal of clamping pressure. They're similar to hand screws that old-time craftsmen once made for themselves. The only advantage that store-bought swivel-nut hand screws have over this traditional design is the ability to clamp surfaces that aren't parallel to each other. However, the shop-made clamps will serve for *most* clamping jobs since nonparallel surfaces and odd angles are the exception in woodworking, not the rule. You can make a dozen traditional hand screws for ordinary work, then purchase a few of the swivel-nut variety for special tasks.

Each of these clamps has two 1-inch-diameter wooden threads and two hardwood jaws. To use the clamp, adjust *both* screws until the jaws just fit over the work. The jaws should be slightly splayed; that is, the tapered ends or tips of the jaws should be farther apart than the square ends. Turn the *inside* screw (the screw in the middle of the jaws) until it's tight — this will squeeze the jaws together near that screw. (The tips still won't contact the work.) Then turn the *outside* screw in the *opposite direction* until tight — this will bring the tips of the jaws together, generating clamping pressure along the length of both jaws.

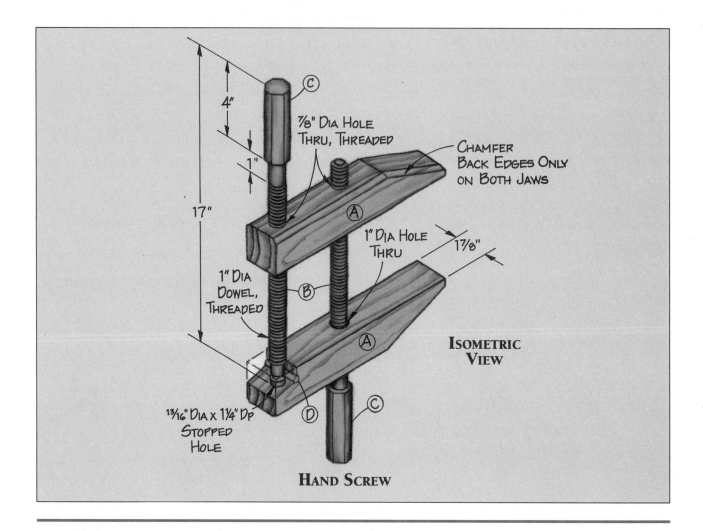

Within the figure:

4"

7/8" DIA HOLE
THRU, THREADED

CHAMFER
BACK EDGES ONLY
ON BOTH JAWS

1"

17"

Ⓐ

1" DIA HOLE
THRU

1 7/8"

1" DIA
DOWEL,
THREADED

Ⓑ

Ⓐ

ISOMETRIC
VIEW

Ⓒ

13/16" DIA. x 1 1/4" DP
STOPPED
HOLE

Ⓓ

Ⓒ

HAND SCREW

MATERIALS LIST (FINISHED DIMENSIONS)

Parts

A. Jaws (2)   1 7/8" x 2 1/4" x 12"
B. Screws (2)   1" dia. x 15"
C. Handles (2)   1 1/2" x 1 1/2" x 4"
D. Pin   3/8" dia. x 1 7/8"

PLAN OF PROCEDURE

1 **Cut the parts to size.** Select clear 8/4 (eight-quarters) hardwood for the jaws and 1-inch-diameter hardwood dowel stock for the screws — maple, oak, and ash all work well. The hand screws shown are made from ash, with maple dowels and walnut handles. Cut the parts to the sizes shown in the Materials List.

2 **Drill holes in the handles and jaws.** Bore 1-inch diameter, 2-inch-deep holes in one end of each handle — these will hold the screws. Drill two 7/8-inch-diameter holes through the first jaw. In the second, drill a 1-inch-diameter hole through and a 13/16-inch-diameter hole 1 1/4 inch deep. Also drill a 3/8-inch-diameter hole perpendicular to the stopped hole, as shown in the *Captured Screw End Detail*.

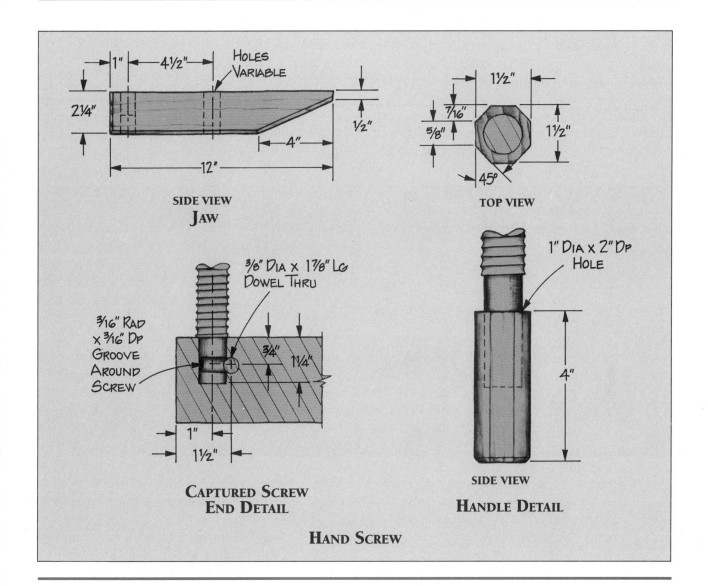

SIDE VIEW
JAW

TOP VIEW

**CAPTURED SCREW
END DETAIL**

SIDE VIEW
HANDLE DETAIL

HAND SCREW

3 Thread the screws and one jaw. Cut threads along 12 inches of each screw, leaving 3 inches at the end of the dowel unthreaded. Also, thread both ^{7}/$_8$-inch-diameter holes in the first jaw.

4 Rout a groove in the end of one screw. On the assembled clamp, the end of one screw is captured in the jaw by a dowel pin. Rout a smooth area on the end of this screw, then rout a ^{3}/$_{16}$-inch-radius, ^{3}/$_{16}$-inch-deep groove in this same area.

5 Taper, bevel, and chamfer the handles and jaws. Cut bevels in the handles to make them octagonal, as shown in the *Handle Detail/Top View.* Cut long tapers in the jaws, as shown in the *Jaw/Side View,* and chamfer the *back* arrises of each jaw.

6 Finish and assemble the clamp. Finish sand the parts of the hand screw, then glue the screws into their handles. Wait for the glue to dry and apply several coats of tung oil to all the wooden parts. Insert the screw *without* the groove through the 1-inch-diameter hole in the second jaw and thread it into the first. (The screw handle will bear against the second jaw as you tighten the screw.) Continue turning the screw until the jaws come together. Thread the other screw through the first jaw and keep turning it until the grooved end rests in the ^{13}/$_{16}$-inch-diameter stopped hole in the second jaw. Drive the ^{3}/$_8$-inch-diameter dowel pin through the second jaw, capturing the end of the screw. **Note:** Don't glue the dowel pin in the jaw, in case you have to replace or repair the screw.

Pipe Clamp

These pipe clamps work in much the same manner as their store-bought counterparts, but they offer two important advantages. First, the assembled clamp sits flat on the workbench and will not roll over. Second, because the jaws are made from laminated plywood and hardwood, you don't need to bother with cauls.

To use this clamp, adjust the position of the tail by loosening the knob and sliding the tail along the pipe. Tighten the knob to lock the tail in place, then assemble the parts in the clamp (or place the clamp over the assembled parts) and turn the handle on the head.

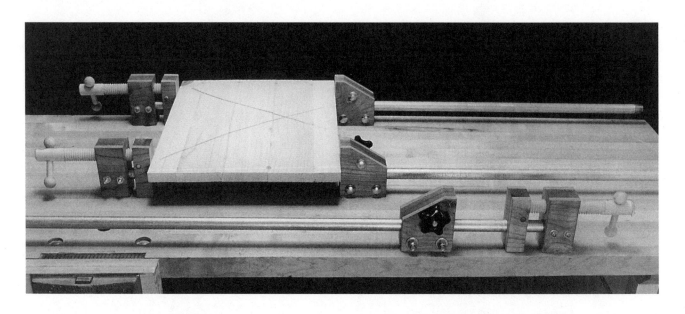

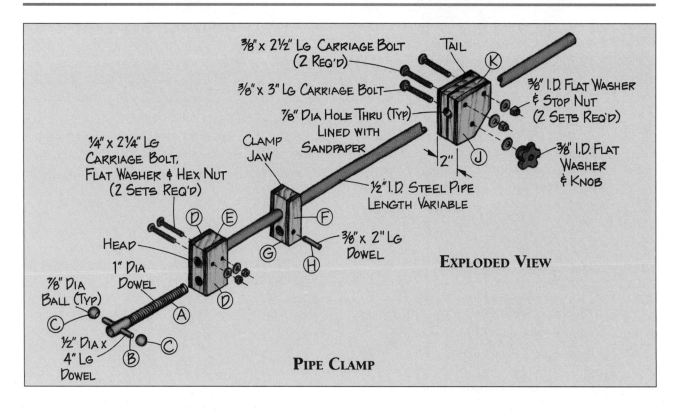

⅜" x 2½" Lg Carriage Bolt (2 Req'd)

⅜" x 3" Lg Carriage Bolt

⅞" Dia Hole Thru (Typ) Lined with Sandpaper

Tail

Ⓚ

⅜" I.D. Flat Washer & Stop Nut (2 Sets Req'd)

⅜" I.D. Flat Washer & Knob

Ⓙ

2"

¼" x 2¼" Lg Carriage Bolt, Flat Washer & Hex Nut (2 Sets Req'd)

Clamp Jaw

Ⓓ Ⓔ

Ⓕ

½" I.D. Steel Pipe Length Variable

Head

Ⓖ

Ⓗ

⅜" x 2" Lg Dowel

1" Dia Dowel

Ⓓ

Exploded View

⅞" Dia Ball (Typ)

Ⓒ

½" Dia x 4" Lg Dowel

Ⓑ

Ⓒ

Ⓐ

Pipe Clamp

MATERIALS LIST (FINISHED DIMENSIONS)

Parts

A. Screw   1″ dia. x 8″
B. Handle   ½″ dia. x 4″
C. Balls (2)   ⅞″ dia.
D. Head sides* (2)   ⅜″ x 2″ x 4″
E. Head center   1¼″ x 2″ x 4″
F. Jaw sides* (2)   ⅜″ x 1¼″ x 4″
G. Jaw center   1¼″ x 1¼″ x 4″
H. Pin   ⅜″ dia. x 2″
J. Tail sides* (2)   ⅜″ x 3¾″ x 4″
K. Tail center   1¼″ x 3¾″ x 4″

Make these parts from plywood.

Hardware

¼″ x 2¼″ Carriage bolts (2)
¼″ Flat washers (2)
¼″ Hex nuts (2)
⅜″ x 2½″ Carriage bolts (2)
⅜″ x 3″ Carriage bolt
⅜″ Flat washers (3)
⅜″ Stop nuts (2)
⅜″ Knob
½″ I.D. Steel pipe (can be any length; does not have to be threaded)
100-grit Aluminum oxide sandpaper (1 sheet)

PLAN OF PROCEDURE

1 Cut the parts to size. Gather the wood and hardware. Note that the pipe does *not* have to be threaded; this helps keep the cost of materials low. Use hardwood plywood for the sides and a dense hardwood (such as maple, oak, or ash) for the centers. The clamps shown are made from birch plywood and maple.

Cut the dowels to length, and plane the hardwood to 1¼ inches thick. Cut one piece of hardwood and two pieces of plywood, each 4¼ inches wide and 8 inches long. Glue these together face-to-face with the plywood on the outside, as shown in the *Head/End View.* Let the glue dry, then cut this laminated stock to make the head, jaw, and tail.

2 Drill holes in the head, jaw, tail, screw, and pipe. Lay out the locations of the holes on the head, jaw, tail, and screw, then drill:
■ ⅞ -inch-diameter holes through the head, jaw, and tail, as shown in the *Head/End View, Jaw/End View,* and *Tail/End View*
■ A ⅞-inch-diameter, ⅞-inch-deep hole in the jaw, as shown in the *Jaw/End View*
■ A ½-inch-diameter hole through the screw, as shown in the *Screw Detail*
■ ⅜ -inch-diameter holes through the tail and the jaw, as shown in the *Screw End Detail* and *Tail/Side View*
■ A ¹³/₃₂-inch-diameter hole through the tail, as shown in the *Tail/Side View*

Insert the pipe in the top ⅞-inch-diameter hole in the head (the hole that won't be threaded). Make sure the

end of the pipe is flush with the end of the head, then drill two ¼-inch-diameter holes through both the head and the pipe, as shown in the *Head/Side View.*

3 Cut the threads in the head and on the screw. Cut threads on the screw stock, starting at the end farthest away from the ½-inch-diameter hole. Leave 2 inches of the stock unthreaded. Cut matching threads in the bottom ⅞-inch-diameter hole in the head.

4 Rout a groove in the end of the screw. On the assembled clamp, the end of the screw is captured in the jaw by a dowel pin. Rout a smooth area on the end of the screw, then rout a ⅜-inch-diameter, ³/₁₆-inch-deep groove in this same area, as shown in the *Screw Detail.*

5 Cut the shape of the tail. Using a band saw or a hand saw, bevel one corner of the tail, as shown in the *Tail/Side View.* Then split the tail down the center, sawing through the ⅞-inch-diameter hole — this hole will form a half-round groove in each half of the tail. Sand the sawed surfaces.

6 Finish and assemble the clamp. Lightly saw the wooden surfaces, then insert the handle through the hole in the screw. Glue a ball to each end of the handle to keep it attached to the handle. (These balls are available from most craft stores and many mail-order woodworking suppliers.) Let the glue dry and apply several coats of tung oil to all wooden parts.

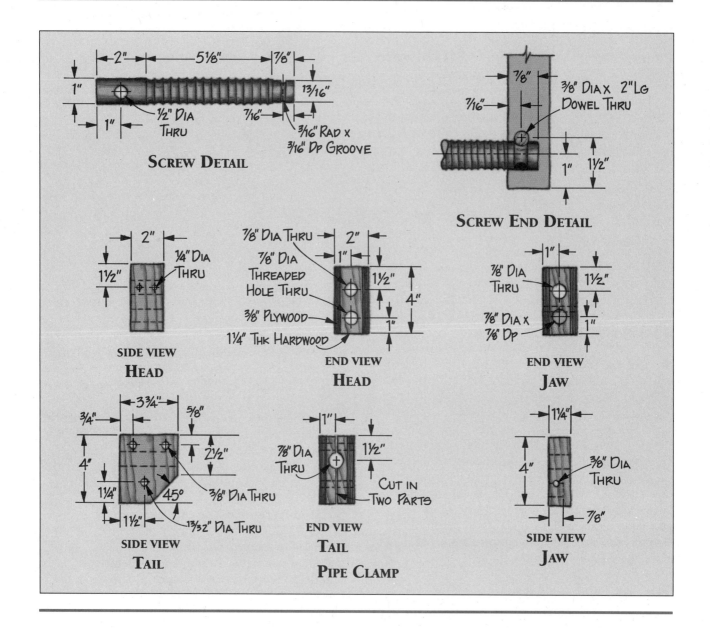

SCREW DETAIL

SCREW END DETAIL

SIDE VIEW
HEAD

END VIEW
HEAD

END VIEW
JAW

SIDE VIEW
TAIL

END VIEW
TAIL
PIPE CLAMP

SIDE VIEW
JAW

Insert the pipe in the head, line up the ¼-inch-diameter holes, and secure the head to the pipe with ¼-inch carriage bolts. Turn the screw into the head and slide the jaw onto the pipe. Insert the grooved end of the screw into the stopped hole in the jaw, and drive the pin into the jaw's ⅜-inch-diameter hole. This will capture the screw in the jaw. (*Don't* glue the pin in place, in case you have to replace or repair the screw.)

Line the half-round grooves in the tail halves with cloth-backed aluminum oxide abrasive, using contact cement to secure the cloth to the wood. Or use aluminum oxide sandpaper, adhering the paper to the wood with glue. (Sandpaper will work fine; it just won't wear as long as cloth-backed abrasives.) *Don't*

use self-adhesive sandpapers; the adhesive won't hold for this application.

Lightly sand the length of pipe to remove any burrs or rough spots. Put the two halves of the tail together, line up the holes, and insert ⅜-inch carriage bolts through the holes. Turn the stop nuts and knob onto the bolts, but don't tighten them yet. Slide the tail onto the pipe and tighten the stop nuts until the tail is snug on the pipe. Loosen each stop nut a fraction of a turn until the tail slides easily along the pipe, then tighten the knob. This should secure the tail so it won't slide. If the tail still slides, readjust the stop nuts. The tail should slide when the knob is loose, but it must remain in place when the knob is tight.

CAM CLAMP

This adjustable bar clamp uses a cam to press the movable jaw against the stock. The jaw moves only about ¼ inch when you throw the cam, but this is enough to apply sufficient gluing pressure to small and medium-size assemblies.

To use the cam clamp, slide the movable jaw away from the fixed jaw. Position the clamp over the stock and move the jaws together until both are touching the stock. Holding the jaws firmly against the stock, rotate the cam lever until the flat on the cam rests against the underside of the movable jaw.

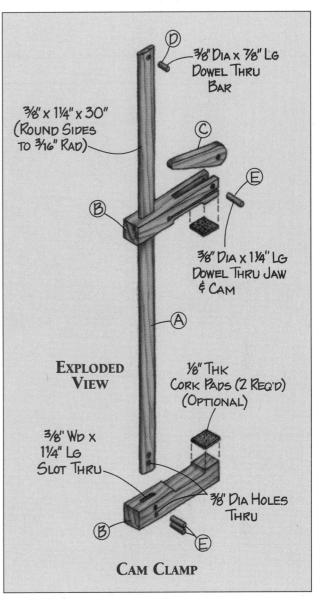

⅜" Dia x ⅞" Lg Dowel Thru Bar

⅜" x 1¼" x 30" (Round Sides to 3/16" Rad)

⅜" Dia x 1¼" Lg Dowel Thru Jaw & Cam

EXPLODED VIEW

⅛" Thk Cork Pads (2 Req'd) (Optional)

⅜" Wd x 1¼" Lg Slot Thru

⅜" Dia Holes Thru

CAM CLAMP

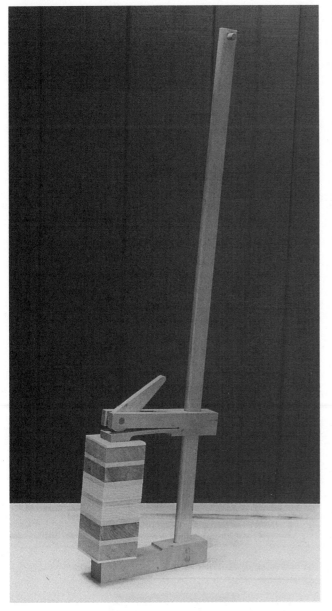

MATERIALS LIST. (FINISHED DIMENSIONS)

Parts

A.	Bar	⅜" x 1¼" x 30"
B.	Jaws (2)	1¼" x 1¼" x 7"
C.	Cam	⅜" x 1¼" x 4¼"
D.	Stop	⅜" dia. x ⅞"
E.	Pins (3)	⅜" dia. x 1¼"

Hardware

⅛" x 1¼" x 1¼" Cork pad
  (2–optional)

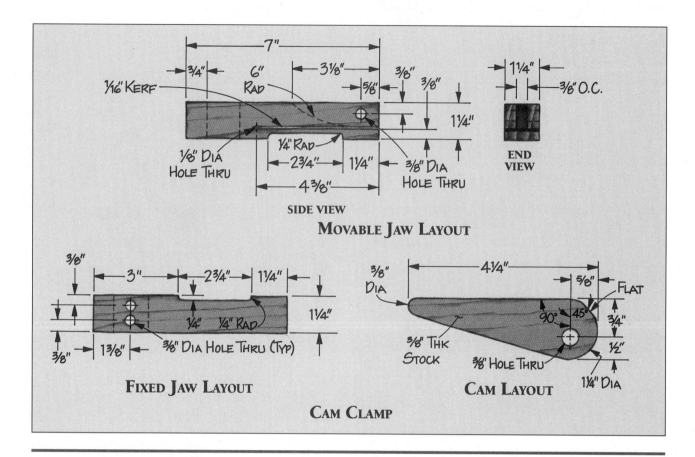

MOVABLE JAW LAYOUT

FIXED JAW LAYOUT

CAM LAYOUT

CAM CLAMP

PLAN OF PROCEDURE

1 Cut the stock to size.   Select a piece of clear, straight-grained 6/4 (six-quarters) or 8/4 (eight-quarters) hardwood and plane it to 1¼ inches thick. Cut the bar, jaws, and cam from this stock. Cut the stop and pins from ⅜-inch-diameter dowel stock.

2 Drill the holes in the bar, jaws, and cam. Lay out the shapes of the jaws and the cam on the stock, and mark the positions of the holes. Then drill:
  ■ A ⅜-inch-diameter hole through the bar, near one end, to hold the stop
  ■ A ⅜-inch-diameter hole through the cam, as shown in the *Cam Layout*
  ■ A ⅜-inch-diameter hole through the movable jaw, as shown in the *Movable Jaw Layout/Side View*
  ■ A ⅛-inch-diameter hole through the movable jaw. Do *not* drill the ⅜-inch-diameter holes in the fixed jaw just yet; wait until you assemble the clamp.

3 Cut the slots in the jaws.   Cut ⅜-inch-wide, 1¼-inch-long slots in the jaws to fit the bar. There are

two possible techniques you might use to make these slots. You can drill a series of overlapping ⅜-inch-diameter holes to rough out the slots, then smooth the sides with a chisel. Or rout the slots with a ⅜-inch straight bit and a table-mounted router.

You must cut two additional slots in the movable jaw. Using a dado cutter, make a ⅜-inch-wide, 3⅛-inch long blind groove in the end of the jaw, as shown in the *Movable Jaw Layout/End View* and *Side View*. This groove will hold the cam. (The dado cutter will leave a radius on the blind end of the groove, but that's okay — it won't interfere with the operation of the cam.) Then cut a ¹⁄₁₆-inch-wide kerf from the end of the jaw to the ⅛-inch-diameter hole with a band saw or a handsaw, as shown in the *Movable Jaw Layout/Side View*. This kerf allows the cam to flex the movable jaw.

4 Cut the shapes of the jaws and cam.   Cut the shapes of the jaws and the cams with a band saw, scroll saw, or coping saw. Sand the sawed surfaces. Also, sand or file a flat area about ⅜ inch long on the cam, as shown in the *Cam Layout*.

5 **Round over the edges of the bar.**   Using a ¼-inch round-over bit and a table-mounted router, round over the edges of the bar. Sand or file the inside surfaces of the slots in the jaws to fit the bar to them. The bar should be snug in the fixed jaw, but it should slide easily through the movable one.

6 **Finish and assemble the clamp.**   Lightly sand the wood surfaces. Insert the bar in the fixed jaw and drill two ⅜-inch-diameter holes through both the jaw

and the bar so you can pin the pieces together. Glue the bar and the pins in the jaw.

Let the glue dry, then place the movable jaw over the bar. Insert the cam in the movable jaw and secure it with a pin and glue. Be careful not to get any glue on the cam; it must rotate freely. Also glue the stop in the bar.

When the glue dries on all the parts, apply several coats of tung oil to the assembled clamp. If you wish, attach cork pads to the jaws with glue.

EXPANDER

While most clamps are designed to press boards together as they're glued to one another, every now and again you need to take glued-up assemblies apart. When you do, this expander may come in handy. It's designed to push two wooden parts away from one another. It also comes in handy as a spreader and a hold-down.

To use the expander, turn the hollow shafts, decreasing the length of the jig so the jaws fit between the parts you want to take apart. Position the expander and turn the shafts in the opposite direction, *increasing* the length of the jig so the jaws press firmly against the parts. Continue to turn the shafts, applying more pressure until the joints come apart.

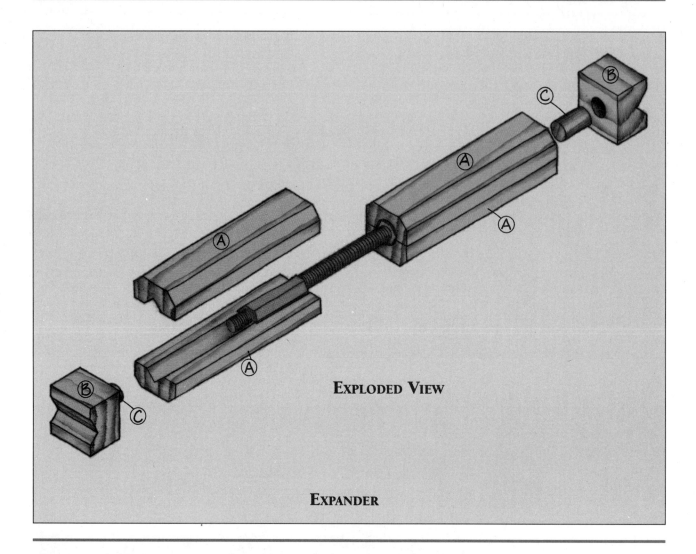

EXPLODED VIEW

EXPANDER

MATERIALS LIST (FINISHED DIMENSIONS)

Parts

A. Shaft halves (4) $\frac{3}{4}''$ x $1\frac{1}{2}''$ x $5''$
B. Jaws (2) $1''$ x $1\frac{1}{2}''$ x $1\frac{1}{2}''$
C. Pins (2) $\frac{1}{2}''$ dia. x $1''$

Hardware

$\frac{3}{8}''$-16 x $8\frac{1}{2}''$ Threaded rod
$\frac{3}{8}''$ Coupling nuts (2)

PLAN OF PROCEDURE

1 Prepare the stock.   Select 4/4 (four-quarters) hardwood for the shaft halves, 5/4 (five-quarters) or thicker hardwood for the jaws, and ½-inch-diameter hardwood dowels for the pins. Plane the shaft stock to ¾ inch thick and the jaw stock to 1 inch thick. Rip both to 1½ inches wide, but do not cut the shaft halves or the jaws to length yet — leave the stock long. Cut the pins to the sizes given in the Materials List.

2 Drill holes in the jaws and shafts.   Test fit the shafts, clamping the halves together. In one end of each shaft, drill a ¾-inch-diameter hole, 1¾ inches deep. (Later you will mount the coupling nuts in these stopped holes.) Also drill ½-inch-diameter, ½-inch-deep holes in the jaws, as shown in the *Expander Section/Side View*. Remove the clamps and take the shaft halves apart.

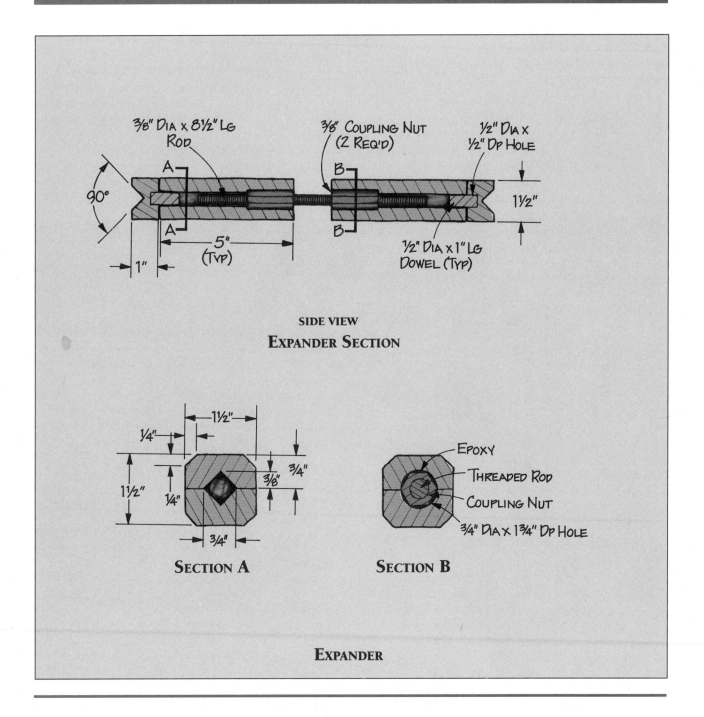

SIDE VIEW

EXPANDER SECTION

SECTION A   **SECTION B**

EXPANDER

3 **Cut chamfers and grooves in the shaft halves and jaws.** Tilt the blade on your table saw or radial arm saw to 45 degrees and chamfer the arrises of the shaft halves, as shown in *Section A*. Leave the blade tilted and cut the V-grooves in the shaft halves and the jaws. Or rout the chamfers and the V-groove with a table-mounted router and a ³/₄-inch-diameter V-groove bit.

4 **Finish and assemble the expander.** Lightly sand the wooden parts, then glue the shaft halves together and glue the pins in the jaws. Apply several coats of tung oil to the assemblies. When the finish dries, glue the coupling nuts in the shaft with epoxy. Be careful not to get any epoxy on the insides of the nuts; you don't want to foul the threads. Turn the threaded rod into both coupling nuts, joining the shafts. Insert the jaw pins into the other ends of the shafts.

MITER CLAMP

This clamp is designed to assemble a miter joint or hold the corners of a box assembly. It applies pressure from *two* directions, holding the parts square to one another. It grips these parts so the joint remains accessible, allowing you to reinforce the joint with nails or other fasteners while it's still in the clamp. It can also be used to square up an assembly and hold the parts in alignment while the glue dries.

To use the miter clamp, back the jaws away from the corner block as far as possible. Adjust the position of the corner block so the stock fits between the block and the jaws. Loosen the wing nuts and slide the jaw assemblies sideways until they are directly across from the corner block. Tighten the wing nuts, place the stock against the corner block, and tighten the jaws.

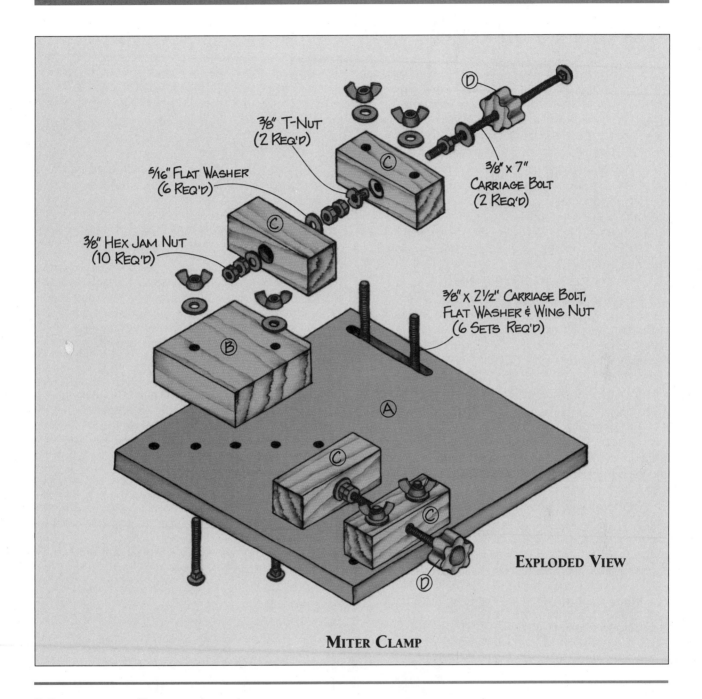

3/8" T-NUT
(2 REQ'D)

5/16" FLAT WASHER
(6 REQ'D)

3/8" x 7"
CARRIAGE BOLT
(2 REQ'D)

3/8" HEX JAM NUT
(10 REQ'D)

3/8" x 2½" CARRIAGE BOLT,
FLAT WASHER & WING NUT
(6 SETS REQ'D)

EXPLODED VIEW

MITER CLAMP

MATERIALS LIST (FINISHED DIMENSIONS)

Parts

A. Base*   ¾" x 12" x 12"
B. Corner block   1½" x 4" x 4"
C. Jaws/nut
    blocks (4)   1½" x 1½" x 4"
D. Knobs (2)   1½" dia. x ¾"

*Make this part from plywood or par-
ticleboard.

Hardware

3/8" x 7" Carriage bolts (2)
3/8" x 2½" Carriage bolts (6)
3/8" T-nuts (2)
3/8" Wing nuts (6)
3/8" Hex jam nuts (10)
3/8" Flat washers (6)
5/16" Flat washers (6)

PLAN OF PROCEDURE

1 Cut the parts to size. Select a scrap of hardwood plywood or particleboard to make the base; clear 8/4 (eight-quarters) hardwood to make the corner block, nut blocks, and jaws; and 4/4 (four-quarters) hardwood to make the knobs. The miter clamp shown is made from medium density fiberboard (MDF) and maple. Plane the 8/4 stock to 1½ inches thick and the 4/4 stock to ¾ inch thick. Cut the parts to the sizes given in the Materials List, except for the knobs. Cut the knob blanks 2½ inches square.

2 Drill holes in the base, corner block, jaws, and nut blocks. Lay out the slots and holes on the base, corner block, jaws, and nut blocks. Then drill:
- A ⁷⁄₁₆-inch-diameter hole with a 1-inch-diameter, ¹⁄₁₆-inch-deep counterbore in each nut block, as shown in the *Nut Block Layout/Top View*
- ³⁄₈-inch-diameter holes with 1-inch-diameter, ¼-inch-deep counterbores, as shown in the *Base Layout/Bottom View*
- A ³⁄₈-inch-diameter hole with a 1-inch-diameter, ⁵⁄₈-inch-deep counterbore in each jaw, as shown in the *Jaw Layout/Top View*
- ³⁄₈-inch-diameter holes through the nut blocks and corner block, as shown in the *Nut Block Layout/Top View* and *Corner Block Layout/Top View*

3 Rout slots in the base. Using a table-mounted router and a ³⁄₈-inch-diameter straight bit, rout two ³⁄₈-inch-wide, 4-inch-long slots in the base, as shown in the *Base Layout/Bottom View*. Change to a 1-inch-diameter bit and rout counterbores for each slot.

4 Make the knobs. Stack the knob blanks face-to-face and tape them together. Lay out the shape of a knob on the top of the stack, as shown in the *Knob Layout*. Drill a ³⁄₈-inch-diameter hole through the center of the stack, then drill additional holes around the circumference of the knob layout to form the indentations. *(SEE FIGURE 7-12.)* Cut the circumference of the knobs with a band saw or scroll saw, and file or sand the sawed surfaces, blending the indentations into the outside edges of the knobs. Take the stack apart and discard the tape.

5 Finish and assemble the clamp. Lightly sand all the wooden parts and apply several coats of tung oil. Let the finish dry, then insert the 7-inch-long carriage bolts through the holes in the knobs and secure the knobs with flat washers and jam nuts. **Note:** Use ⁵⁄₁₆-inch-diameter washers for the jaw assemblies. These smaller washers will fit over the ³⁄₈-inch-diameter bolts and inside the jaw counterbores.

Mount the T-nuts in the nut blocks and thread the carriage bolts through the T-nuts. Thread two jam nuts and a washer onto each carriage bolt, then slip the jaws over the ends of the bolts. Place another washer and two more jam nuts onto each bolt. Position these last two jam nuts so they are at the very ends of the bolts, and tighten them against one another. Pull the jaws toward these nuts until the washer and both nuts slip into the counterbore in the jaw. Turn the other set of jam nuts up against the jaw, back them off about half a turn, and tighten them against each other. The jam nuts will hold the jaws on the ends of the bolts, yet allow the jaws to turn freely.

Using 2½-inch-long carriage bolts, washers, and wing nuts, fasten the jaw assemblies and the corner block to the base.

7-10 To make the knob shape, first scribe a circle to mark the circumference of the knob. Then drill a ³⁄₈-inch-diameter hole every 60 degrees around the circumference — these holes will form the indentations in the knob. Cut the circumference with a band saw or scroll saw. Using a file or sandpaper, blend the indentations and the edges of the knobs so there are no sharp corners.

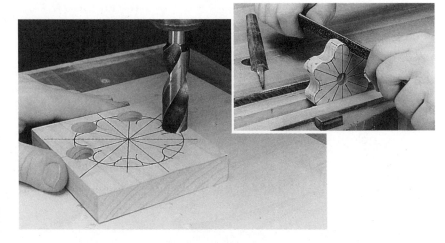

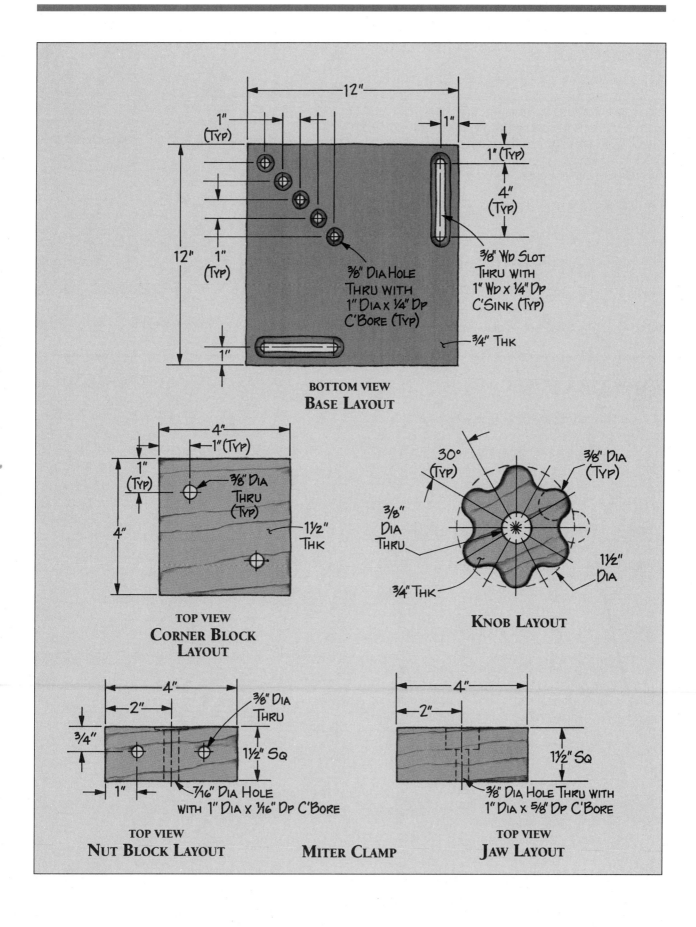

12"

1"
(Typ)

1"

1" (Typ)

4"
(Typ)

12"

1"
(Typ)

1"

³⁄₈" Dia Hole
Thru with
1" Dia x ¹⁄₄" Dp
C'Bore (Typ)

³⁄₈" Wd Slot
Thru with
1" Wd x ¹⁄₄" Dp
C'Sink (Typ)

³⁄₄" Thk

BOTTOM VIEW
BASE LAYOUT

4"

1" (Typ)

1"
(Typ)

³⁄₈" Dia
Thru
(Typ)

1¹⁄₂"
Thk

4"

TOP VIEW
CORNER BLOCK
LAYOUT

30°
(Typ)

³⁄₈" Dia
(Typ)

³⁄₈"
Dia
Thru

1¹⁄₂"
Dia

³⁄₄" Thk

KNOB LAYOUT

4"

2"

³⁄₄"

³⁄₈" Dia
Thru

1¹⁄₂" Sq

1"

⁷⁄₁₆" Dia Hole
with 1" Dia x ¹⁄₁₆" Dp C'Bore

TOP VIEW
NUT BLOCK LAYOUT

4"

2"

1¹⁄₂" Sq

³⁄₈" Dia Hole Thru with
1" Dia x ⁵⁄₈" Dp C'Bore

TOP VIEW
JAW LAYOUT

MITER CLAMP

Violin Clamp

You don't always need a clamp with a long reach or a large capacity. Many gluing operations require nothing but a simple device to squeeze two wooden parts together. This violin clamp will handle the job nicely. Although its small size makes it a light-duty clamp, you can generate a surprising amount of pressure. It's also very useful for holding assemblies to a clamping grid.

To use the clamp, loosen the wing nut and pull the circular jaws apart. Fit the jaws over the assembly you wish to clamp, then tighten the wing nut.

Plan of Procedure

1 **Cut the parts to size.** Make the jaws from hardwood plywood — if you make them from solid wood, they may split. (The violin clamp shown is made from birch plywood.) Cut the circular jaws with a 2¼-inch-diameter hole saw — the plug that the saw cuts will be approximately 2 inches in diameter. Sand the sawed edges.

Note: You may be tempted to make the jaws larger than 2 inches in diameter to increase the reach of the clamp. Unfortunately, this will do little good. The jaws tilt slightly when you tighten the wing nut. Because of this, they only generate pressure in the immediate vicinity of the carriage bolt. Larger jaws will not spread the pressure out over a broader area.

2 **Enlarge the holes in the jaws.** The pilot bit on the hole saw will leave a small hole in the center of each jaw, but this hole won't be large enough to fit over a ⅜-inch-diameter bolt. Using a drill press and a ⅜-inch-diameter twist bit, enlarge the hole in each jaw. To safely hold the jaw as you drill it, either clamp it in a hand screw or hold it with large slip-jaw pliers.

3 **Finish and assemble the clamp.** Lightly sand the jaws and apply several coats of tung oil. Wait for the finish to dry, then insert a carriage bolt through both jaws. Secure the jaws on the bolt with a fender washer and a wing nut.

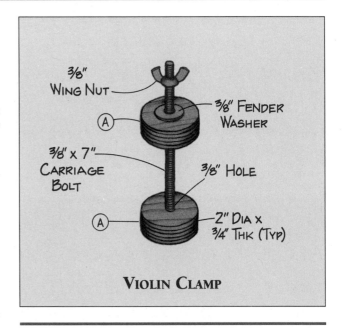

VIOLIN CLAMP

Materials List (FINISHED DIMENSIONS)
Parts

A. Jaws (2)   2″ dia. x ¾″

Hardware

⅜″ x 7″ Carriage bolt
⅜″ Fender washer
⅜″ Flat washer
⅜″ Wing nut

HOLD-DOWN

Not only do you need clamps to hold wooden parts as you glue them together, you must sometimes clamp the parts to the workbench as you work on them. This hold-down is designed for that task. It can be mounted anywhere on your workbench, using existing bench dog holes. Or you can drill a set of mounting holes just for this purpose. To use the fixture, place the board you want to clamp to the bench top under the small end of the hold-down and tighten the knob.

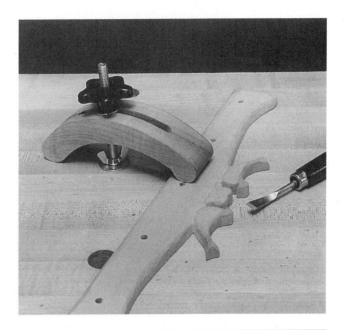

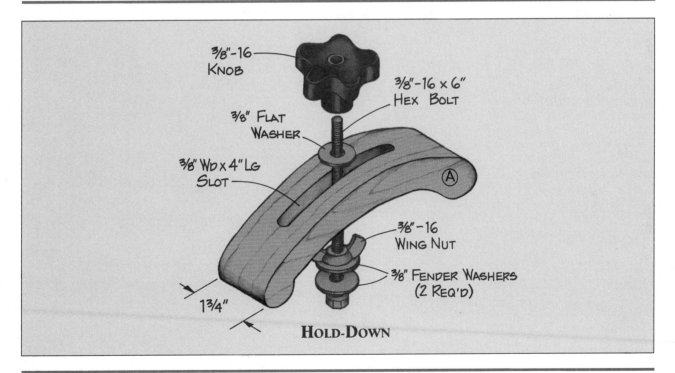

HOLD-DOWN

MATERIALS LIST (FINISHED DIMENSIONS)

Parts

A. Hold-down 1¾" x 2⅜" x 7"

Hardware

⅜" x 6" Hex bolt
⅜" Flat washer
⅜" Fender washers (2)
⅜" Knob
⅜" Wing nut

PLAN OF PROCEDURE

1 **Cut the shape of the hold-down.** Select a clear, straight-grained piece of 8/4 (eight-quarters) hardwood to make the hold-down and plane it to 1¾ inches thick. Lay out the shape of the hold-down on the stock and cut it with a band saw or coping saw. Sand the sawed edges.

2 **Cut the slot in the hold-down.** With the *convex* side of the hold-down resting on the table of your drill press, bore two ⅜-inch-diameter holes through it to mark the beginning and end of the slot. Remove the waste between the holes with a scroll saw or a coping saw. *(SEE FIGURE 7-11.)*

3 **Finish and assemble the hold-down.** Lightly sand the hold-down and apply several coats of tung oil. As the finish dries, select a bench dog hole in your workbench to mount the hold-down. If you don't have a suitable hole at least ⅜ inch in diameter, drill one. You may want to drill several holes so you can mount the hold-down in different locations on the bench.

When the finish is dry, place a fender washer over a ⅜-inch-diameter, 6-inch-long hex bolt, insert it up through the bench-top hole you've selected, and secure it with another fender washer and a wing nut. Place the hold-down over the bolt, move the stock you want to clamp down under the small end of the hold-down, and secure it with a flat washer and a knob, as shown in the *Hold-Down Mounting Detail*.

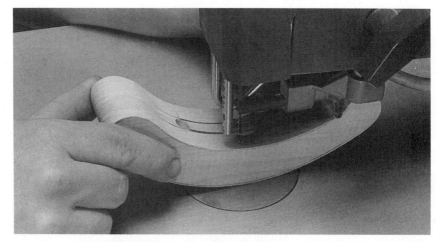

7-11 To create the slot in the hold-down, first drill two holes to mark the ends of the slot. Then make an interior cut with a scroll saw or coping saw — insert the blade through one hole and cut out the waste between holes. Do this with the convex side of the hold-down on the saw table. Slowly rotate or rock the hold-down as you cut to keep it firmly against the table.

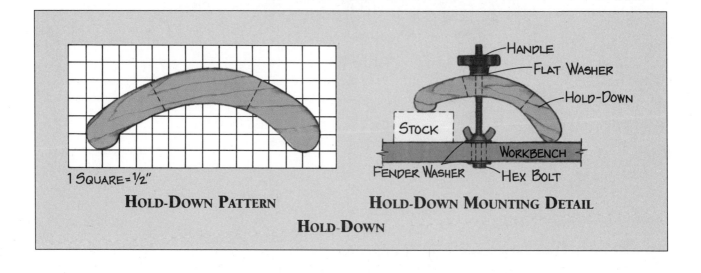

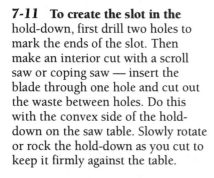

1 SQUARE = ½"

HOLD-DOWN PATTERN

HANDLE
FLAT WASHER
HOLD-DOWN
STOCK
WORKBENCH
FENDER WASHER — HEX BOLT

HOLD-DOWN MOUNTING DETAIL

HOLD-DOWN

CLAMPING PRESS

This unique press generates pressure from *two* directions. Like a common veneer press, it will apply pressure downward, across a broad surface. However, it also presses in from one side. This feature makes it doubly useful. Not only can you apply veneer to panels and laminate boards face-to-face but you can also use the press to glue up wide stock and butcherblocks. By using the overhead clamps to press the boards against the base as you glue them edge to edge, you can make perfectly flat panels.

To use the jig to apply vertical clamping pressure, slide the vertical pressure bars along the ledges, positioning the screws over the work. Place thick, wide cauls between the work and the ends of the screws, then turn the knobs to tighten the screws. To apply horizontal pressure, first determine how far above the base to mount the screws. You want the lines of pressure as close to the center of the stock as possible. If the stock is ³/₄ inch thick, mount the screws in the T-nuts that are ³/₈ inch above the base. If the stock is 1¹/₂ inches thick, use the nuts that are ³/₄ inch above it, and so on. When you have positioned the screws, place the horizontal caul between the ends of the screws and the work. Turn the knobs to tighten the screws. If the stock wants to buckle when you apply horizontal pressure, hold it flat with several overhead screws.

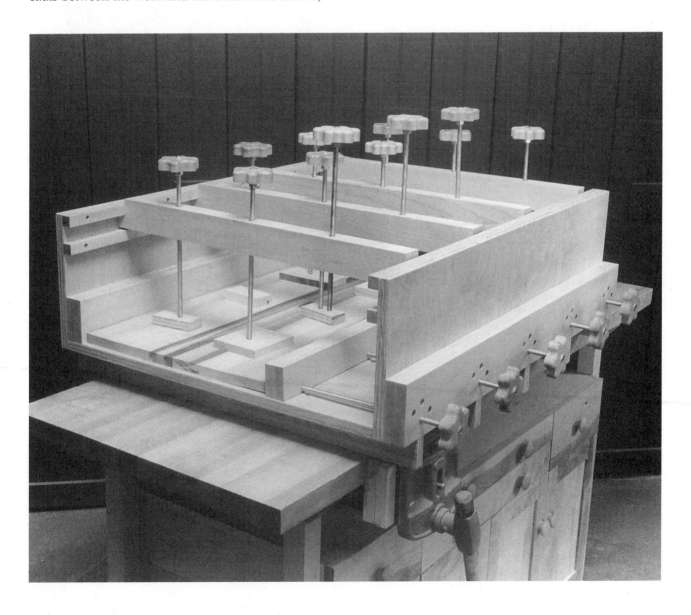

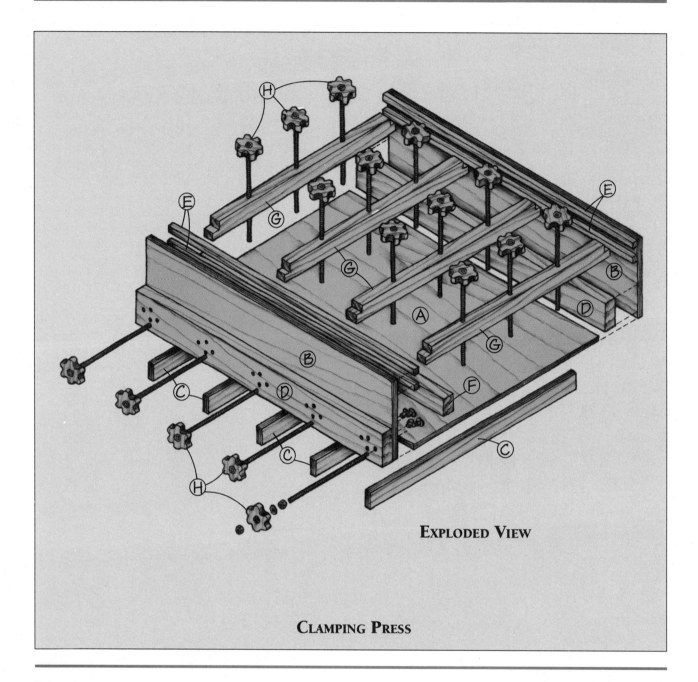

EXPLODED VIEW

CLAMPING PRESS

MATERIALS LIST (FINISHED DIMENSIONS)

Parts

A. Base*   ¾" x 27" x 36"
B. Sides* (2)   ¾" x 10" x 36"
C. Braces* (5)   ¾" x 2" x 30"
D. Support
    blocks (2)   1½" x 3¼" x 36"
E. Ledges (4)   ¾" x ¾" x 36"
F. Horizontal
    caul   1½" x 2¼" x 36"

G. Vertical pressure
    bars (4)   1½" x 2" x 26⅞"
H. Knobs (17)   3" dia. x ¾"

*Make these parts from plywood or par-
ticleboard.

Hardware

⅜"-16 x 11⅞" Threaded rods (17)
⅜" T-nuts (32)
⅜" Hex nuts (34)
⅜" Flat washers (17)
#8 x 1¼" Flathead wood screws
    (42–48)

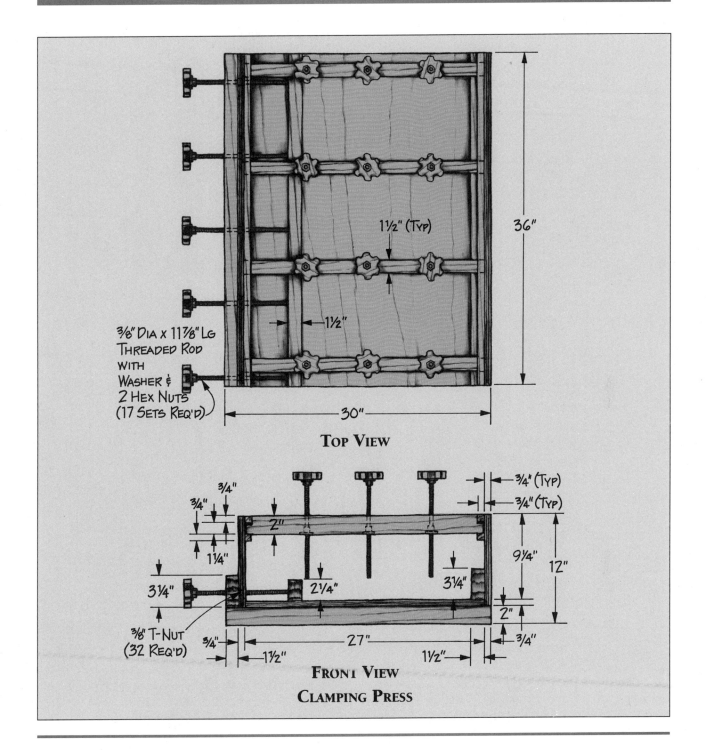

TOP VIEW

FRONT VIEW

CLAMPING PRESS

PLAN OF PROCEDURE

1 Cut the parts to size. Select hardwood plywood or particleboard for the base, braces, and sides; 4/4 (four-quarters) hardwood for the ledges and handles; and 8/4 (eight-quarters) hardwood for the support blocks, caul, and pressure bars. (The press shown is made from birch plywood and solid maple.) Cut the parts to the sizes given in the Materials List, except for the knob stock. Cut these pieces 4 inches square.

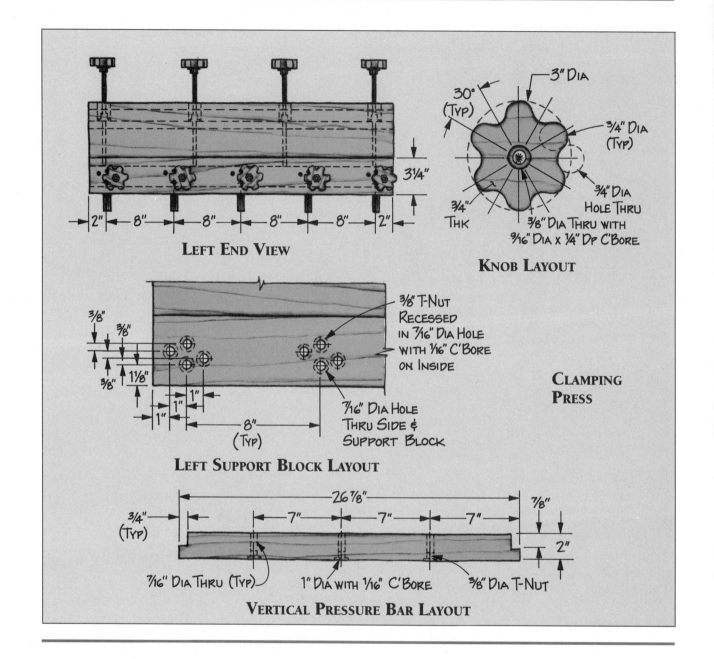

LEFT END VIEW

KNOB LAYOUT

LEFT SUPPORT BLOCK LAYOUT

CLAMPING PRESS

VERTICAL PRESSURE BAR LAYOUT

2   Laminate the left support block and the left side.   Select the left support block and the left side — the parts that will hold the horizontal screw. Glue these two parts together so the ends and the bottom edges are flush.

3   Drill holes in the left side assembly and vertical pressure bars.   Lay out the positions of the T-nuts as shown in the *Vertical Pressure Bar Layout* and *Left Support Block Layout*. Then drill a 1-inch-diameter, $1/16$-inch-deep counterbore and a $7/16$-inch-diameter hole for each T-nut.

4   Notch the ends of the vertical pressure bars.   The ends of the vertical pressure bars must be notched to fit between the ledges, as shown in the *Vertical Pressure Bar Layout*. Mark these notches, then cut them with a band saw or a backsaw.

5   Make the knobs.   Stack three or four knob blanks face-to-face and tape the stack together. Repeat until you have stacked up all the knob blanks in four or five piles. Lay out the shape of the knob on the top blank in each stack, as shown in the *Knob Layout*. Drill $3/4$-inch-diameter holes around the circumference of the knob layout to form the indentations. Cut the circumference of the knobs with a band saw or scroll saw, and file or sand the sawed surfaces, blending the indentations into the edges. As you complete each stack, take it apart and discard the tape. Then drill a 9/16-inch-diameter, 1/4-inch-deep counterbore and a 3/8-inch-diameter hole through the center of each knob.

6 Finish and assemble the press. Lightly sand the wooden parts. Glue the ledges to the sides, let the glue dry, and mount the T-nuts in the left side assembly and the vertical pressure bars. Assemble the left side assembly, right side, base, and remaining support

block with glue and flathead screws. Then glue and screw this assembly to the braces. Be sure to countersink all screws so the heads are slightly below the surface.

Turn a hex nut onto each threaded rod until it's about 1 inch from the end, and place a flat washer over the hex nut. Insert the rod through a knob so the rod protrudes out of the counterbore. Turn another nut onto the rod so this second nut is flush with the rod end. Tighten the first nut against the knob until it draws the second nut into the counterbore. Repeat for each rod and knob. Finally, turn these assemblies into the T-nuts in the vertical pressure bars and left support block.

FRAME CLAMP

This frame clamp uses a single screw to generate pressure on all four corners of a rectangular frame. It's specifically designed to hold *mitered* frames. It not only presses the corners together, but also keeps the miter joints properly aligned until the glue dries.

To use the clamp, loosen the knob and position the brackets so they fit over the frame. The brackets must

be positioned *symmetrically*; that is, each must be in the same position on its respective arm. If necessary, adjust the tension on the compression spring. Place the clamp over the frame and slowly tighten the knob. When the clamp is tight, check that the frame is square.

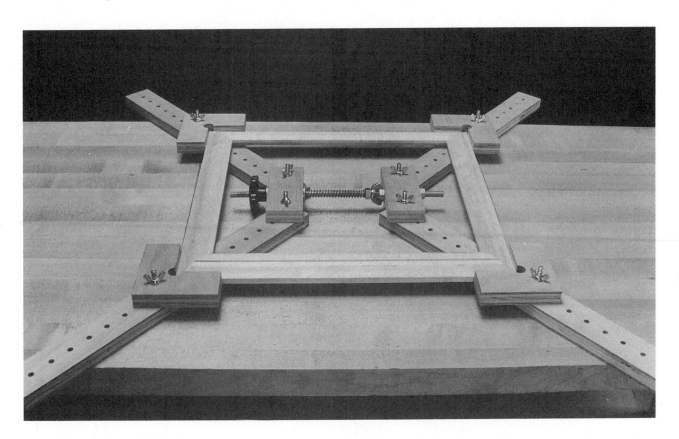

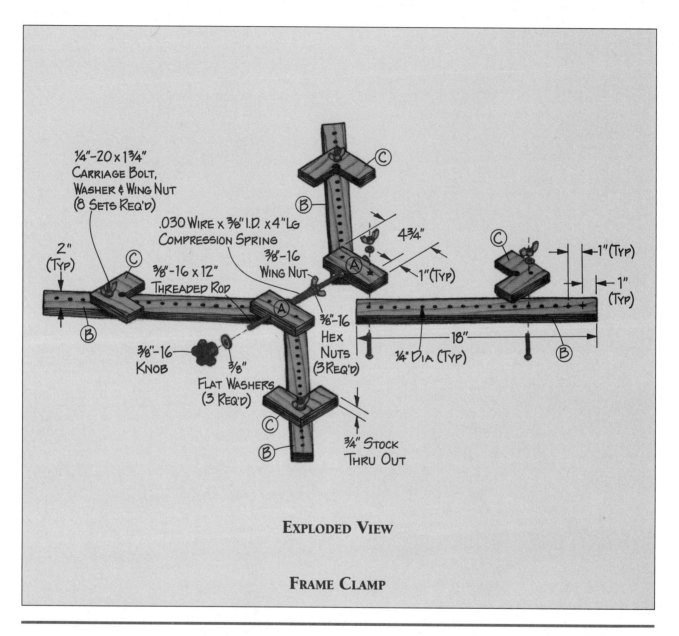

¼"–20 x 1¾"
CARRIAGE BOLT,
WASHER & WING NUT
(8 SETS REQ'D)

.030 WIRE x ⅜" I.D. x 4" LG
COMPRESSION SPRING

⅜"–16
WING NUT

4¾"

1"(TYP)

2"
(TYP)

⅜"–16 x 12"
THREADED ROD

1"(TYP)

1"
(TYP)

⅜"–16
HEX
NUTS
(3 REQ'D)

⅜"–16
KNOB

⅜"
FLAT WASHERS
(3 REQ'D)

18"

¼" DIA (TYP)

¾" STOCK
THRU OUT

EXPLODED VIEW

FRAME CLAMP

MATERIALS LIST (FINISHED DIMENSIONS)

Parts

A. Tie bars (2)   ¾" x 2" x 4¾"
B. Arms (4)   ¾" x 2" x 18"
C. Brackets (4)   ¾" x 4" x 4"

Hardware

¼" x 1¾" Carriage bolts (8)
¼" Flat washers (8)
¼" Wing nuts (8)
⅜"–16 x 12" Threaded rod
⅜" Flat washers (3)
⅜" Hex nuts (3)
⅜" Wing nut
.030 Wire x ⅜" x 4" Compression
   spring
⅜" Knob (2¼" O.D. maximum)

PLAN OF PROCEDURE

1 Cut the parts to size. Select cabinet-grade plywood for all the parts. (The frame clamps shown are made from birch plywood.) Cut the parts to the sizes given in the Materials List.

2 Drill holes in the tie bars, arms, and brackets. Stack all four arms face-to-face with the ends and edges flush, and tape them together. Do the same for the brackets and the tie bars. Mark the locations of the holes on the top part in each stack. Also mark the shape of the bracket on the bracket stack, as shown in the *Bracket/Bottom View*. Then drill:
- ⅝-inch-diameter holes through the brackets, as shown in the *Bracket/Bottom View*
- ¼-inch-diameter holes through the brackets
- ¼-inch-diameter holes through the arms
- ¼-inch-diameter holes through the tie bars

Take apart the tie bar and the arm stacks and discard the tape. (Leave the bracket stack taped together for the time being.) Mark the locations of the ⅜-inch-diameter holes on the edges of the tie bars and drill them.

3 Cut the shapes of the brackets. Cut the bracket shape with a band saw or handsaw, cutting through all four brackets at once. Sand the sawed edges, then take the bracket stack apart and discard the tape. Cut ⅛-inch chamfers on the inside arrises of the brackets.

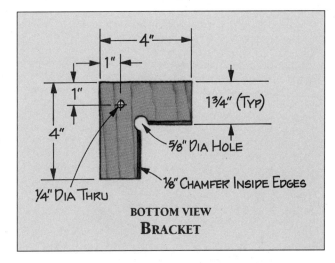

BOTTOM VIEW
BRACKET

4"

1"

1"

4"

¼" DIA THRU

1¾" (TYP)

⅝" DIA HOLE

⅛" CHAMFER INSIDE EDGES

4 Finish and assemble the frame clamp.
Lightly sand all parts and apply several coats of tung oil. Let the finish dry, then insert the threaded rod through the ⅜-inch-diameter hole in one of the tie bars and secure it with hex nuts. Turn a wing nut and the remaining hex nut onto the rod, then slip the compression spring and the flat washer over the rod. Insert the rod through the other tie bar, put another flat washer over the end of the rod, and fasten the bars together with a knob.

Fasten the arms to the tie bars with ¼-inch carriage bolts, flat washers, and wing nuts. Then fasten the brackets to the arm with the remaining hardware.

PANEL CLAMP

If you glue up a lot of wide panels, you'll appreciate this lightweight panel clamp. It generates more than enough pressure to glue boards edge to edge, yet adds very little weight to the assembly. This makes it easy to move the panel around while it's clamped together.

To use the clamp, loosen the wing nuts and remove the top bar. Lay the boards across the bottom bar and position the stop and the cam. (With the boards against the stop and the cam open as far as possible, there should be no more than ½ inch of space between the boards and the cam.) Apply glue to the edges of the boards, align them, replace the top bar, and turn the wing nuts until snug (but *not* tight). Rotate the cam, applying as much pressure as possible, then tighten the wing nut over the cam to hold it in place.

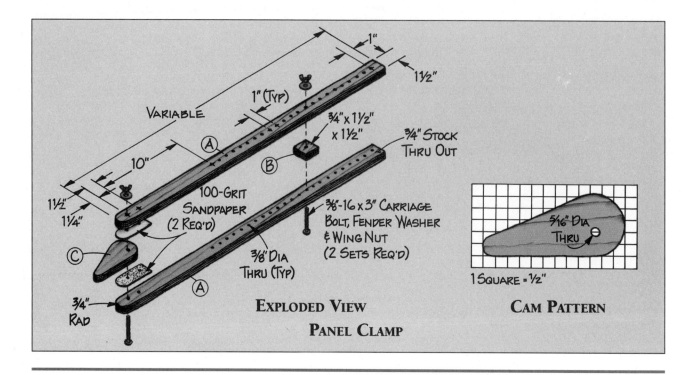

EXPLODED VIEW

PANEL CLAMP

CAM PATTERN

MATERIALS LIST (FINISHED DIMENSIONS)

Parts

A. Bars (2) ³/₄″ x 1½″ x (variable)
B. Stop   ³/₄″ x 1½″ x 1½″
C. Cam   ³/₄″ x 2⅝″ x 6″

Hardware

³/₈″ x 3″ Carriage bolts (2)
³/₈″ Fender washers (2)
³/₈″ Wing nuts (2)
100-grit Sandpaper or emery cloth
  (1 sheet)

PLAN OF PROCEDURE

1 Cut the parts to size. Select cabinet-grade ³/₄-inch plywood to make the parts, then cut them to the sizes given in the Materials List. **Note:** The stop and the cam should be the same thickness or just a little thicker than the stock you wish to glue edge to edge. If you want to glue up stock thinner than ³/₄ inch, make the stop and cam out of thinner plywood. To glue up stock thicker than ³/₄ inch, either make a thicker stop and cam or use washers as spacers.

2 Drill holes in the parts. Stack the bars face-to-face with the edges and ends flush, and tape them together. Lay out the positions of the holes on the top bar. Also lay out the cam and the hole in the stop. Drill ³/₈-inch-diameter holes in the bars, cam, and stop.

3 Cut the shape of the cam and bars. Cut the shape of the cam using a band saw, saber saw, or coping saw. Also cut the radius in the front (cam) end of the bars. Sand the sawed edges, then take the bars apart and discard the tape.

4 Assemble the panel clamp. Lightly sand the wooden parts, and glue 4-inch-long strips of sandpaper or emery cloth to the inside faces of the bars, near the front ends, as shown in the *Exploded View*. Apply several coats of tung oil to all wood surfaces, and wax the bar clamps to keep the glue from sticking. (Be careful not to get any tung oil or wax on the sandpaper.) Assemble the bars, cam, and stop with carriage bolts, washers, and wing nuts.

Long-Reach C-Clamp

Although this isn't the sort of C-clamp you may be used to, it performs the same job. Instead of applying pressure directly to the stock with the screw, as most clamps do, the screw in this clamp draws the two arms of the "C" together to pinch the stock between them. The advantage of this design is that it concentrates the clamping pressure in a very small area rather than spreading it out. It also extends the reach. The throat of this clamp is approximately 7 inches, a good deal deeper than most traditional C-clamps.

To use the clamp, remove the carriage bolt that holds the movable arm to the yoke and adjust the position of the arm. The arms must be far enough apart to just fit over what you want to clamp. Also adjust the tension on the compression spring by loosening the wing nut and turning the hex nut next to it. The tension should be just enough to keep the arms spread. When the movable arm is properly positioned and the spring is adjusted, put the clamp over the stock and tighten the knob.

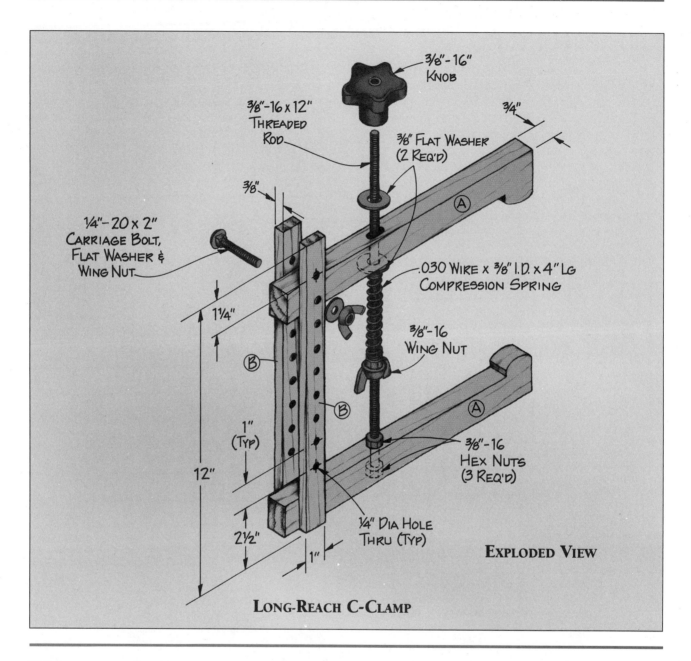

3/8"-16" KNOB

3/8"-16 x 12" THREADED ROD

3/8" FLAT WASHER (2 REQ'D)

3/4"

3/8"

1/4"- 20 x 2" CARRIAGE BOLT, FLAT WASHER & WING NUT

A

.030 WIRE x 3/8" I.D. x 4" LG COMPRESSION SPRING

1 1/4"

B

3/8"-16 WING NUT

B

1" (TYP)

A

3/8"-16 HEX NUTS (3 REQ'D)

12"

1/4" DIA HOLE THRU (TYP)

2 1/2"

1"

EXPLODED VIEW

LONG-REACH C-CLAMP

MATERIALS LIST (FINISHED DIMENSIONS)

Parts

A. Arms (2)   3/4" x 1 1/2" x 12"
B. Yokes (2)   3/8" x 1" x 12"

Hardware

3/8"-16 x 12" Threaded rod
3/8" Flat washers (2)
3/8" Hex nuts (3)
3/8" Wing nut
.030 Wire x 3/8" x 4" Compression spring
1/4" x 2" Carriage bolt
1/4" Flat washer
1/4" Wing nut

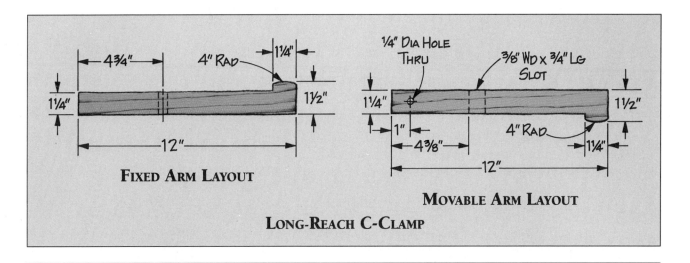

FIXED ARM LAYOUT

MOVABLE ARM LAYOUT

LONG-REACH C-CLAMP

PLAN OF PROCEDURE

1 Cut the parts to size. Select straight-grained, clear hardwood for the arms. The yokes can be made from either hardwood or plywood. (On the clamp shown, the arms are ash and the yokes are birch plywood.) Cut the parts to the sizes given in the Materials List. If you wish to make smaller clamps, reduce the *lengths* of the parts, but leave the thicknesses and widths as stated. If you wish to make larger ones, increase the lengths of all parts and the *widths* of the arms.

2 Drill holes and slots in the yokes and arms. Stack the yokes face-to-face with the ends and edges flush, and tape them together. Lay out the positions of the 1/4-inch-diameter holes on one yoke, spacing the holes evenly along it. Drill the holes through both yokes at the same time.

Drill a 1/4-inch-diameter hole through the movable arm, as shown in the *Movable Arm Layout*. Drill a 3/8-inch-diameter hole through the fixed arm, as shown in the *Fixed Arm Layout*, then cut a 3/8-inch-wide, 3/4-inch-long slot in the movable arm. (*SEE FIGURE 7-12.*)

3 Cut the shapes of the arms. Stack the arms face-to-face with the ends and edges flush. Lay out the arm shape on one face, then cut both arms at once, using a band saw or a saber saw. Sand the sawed surfaces.

4 Finish and assemble the C-clamp. Lightly sand the wooden parts. Insert two 1/4-inch-diameter dowels or bolts through two sets of holes in the yokes to keep them aligned, then glue the yokes to the fixed

arm. When the glue dries, apply several coats of tung oil to all surfaces.

Insert the 3/8-inch threaded rod in the hole in the fixed arm and secure it with hex nuts. Thread the wing nut and the other 3/8-inch hex nut on the rod, then place the compression spring and a 3/8-inch flat washer over the nuts. Fit the movable arm between the yokes and over the rod. Secure the end of the arm to the yokes with a 1/4-inch carriage bolt, flat washer, and wing nut. Place the remaining 3/8-inch flat washer over the rod and thread the knob onto it.

7-12 To make the 3/8-inch-wide, 3/4-inch-long slot in the movable arm, first drill two 3/8-inch-diameter holes side by side. Insert the drill bit in one of the holes and, with the drill running, tilt the bit from side to side. This will remove the waste between the holes and create a slot.

INDEX

Note: Page references in *italic* indicate photographs or illustrations.
Boldface references indicate charts or tables.

WOODWORKING GLOSSARY

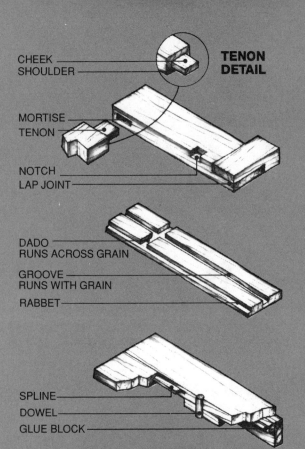

TENON DETAIL

CHEEK
SHOULDER

MORTISE
TENON

NOTCH
LAP JOINT

DADO
RUNS ACROSS GRAIN

GROOVE
RUNS WITH GRAIN

RABBET

SPLINE
DOWEL
GLUE BLOCK

BASIC JOINERY

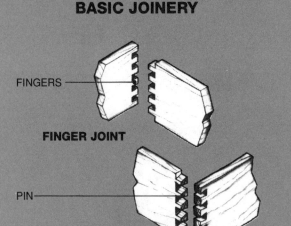

FINGERS

FINGER JOINT

PIN

TAIL

DOVETAIL JOINT

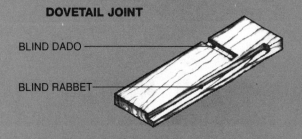

BLIND DADO

BLIND RABBET

SPECIAL JOINERY

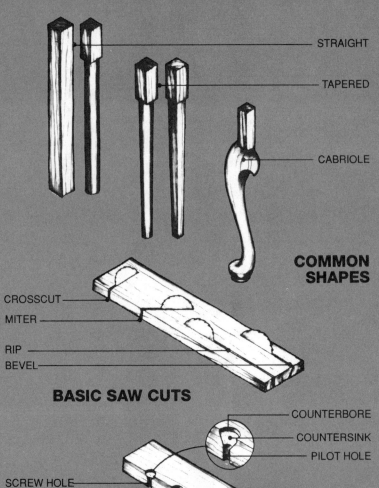

STRAIGHT

TAPERED

CABRIOLE

COMMON SHAPES

CROSSCUT
MITER

RIP
BEVEL

BASIC SAW CUTS

COUNTERBORE
COUNTERSINK
PILOT HOLE

SCREW HOLE
STOPPED HOLE
THRU HOLE

HOLES

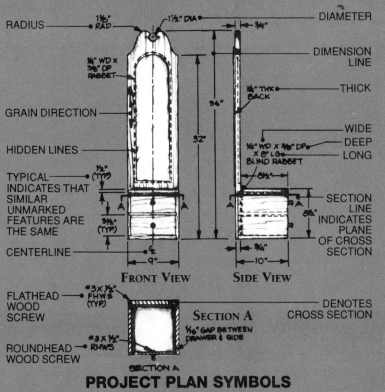

RADIUS
1⅛" RAD
1½" DIA
¾"
DIAMETER

⅛" WD X ⅜" DP RABBET

DIMENSION LINE

⅛" THK BACK

THICK

36"

GRAIN DIRECTION

32"

⅛" WD X ⅜" DP X 8" LG BLIND RABBET

WIDE
DEEP
LONG

HIDDEN LINES

8½"

TYPICAL INDICATES THAT SIMILAR UNMARKED FEATURES ARE THE SAME

½" (TYP)

3½" (TYP)

SECTION LINE INDICATES PLANE OF CROSS SECTION

8½"

CENTERLINE

C

9"

¾"

10"

FRONT VIEW

SIDE VIEW

FLATHEAD WOOD SCREW

#3 X ½" FHWS (TYP)

SECTION A

⅛" GAP BETWEEN DRAWER & SIDE

DENOTES CROSS SECTION

ROUNDHEAD WOOD SCREW

#3 X ½" RHWS

SECTION A

PROJECT PLAN SYMBOLS